A Winning Way:
A Wrestling Coaches Road Map for Success

A Winning Way:
A Wrestling Coaches Road Map for Success

BY
DARREL A. WHITE

www.BookstandPublishing.com

Published by
Bookstand Publishing
Gilroy, CA 95020
2496_7

Copyright © 2008 by Darrel White
All rights reserved. No part of this publication may be reproduced or
transmitted in any form or by any means, electronic or mechanical,
including photocopy, recording, or any information storage and
retrieval system, without permission in writing from the copyright
owner.

ISBN 978-1-58909-568-7

Printed in the United States of America

Contents

Dedication	i
Introduction	ii
Ch 1 Developing a Coaching Philosophy	1
Ch 2 Program Promotion	11
Ch 3 Recruiting	37
Ch 4 Program Building	55
Ch 5 Creating a Season Plan	63
Ch 6 Practices	69
Ch 7 Technique	81
Ch 8 Drilling	95
Ch 9 Conditioning	103
Ch 10 Peaking	119
Ch 11 Dual Meet Strategies	135
Ch 12 Developing Team Leaders	145
Ch 13 Assistant Coaches	157
Ch 14 Boosters	161
Ch 15 Working with Athletic Administrators	167
Ch 16 A Final Reflection	169
Appendix 1 Coaching Philosophy	170
Appendix 2 Season Plan	174

Appendix 3 Practice Plan Modalities	177
Appendix 4 Strict-Drill Sequence	179
Appendix 5 Boosters Club Constitution and Bylaws	182
Citations and Credits	184
About the Author	185

Dedication

Without the amazing support of my wife and our children I could never have achieved longevity as a coach. Thank you Linda, Glen, Chance and Glee. Your love, assistance, confidence and sacrifice allowed me to pursue my dreams with four able co-pilots.

I am also deeply indebted to the many talented, hard-working assistants, capable administrators and mentor coaches whose influence helped me to chart and successfully navigate the waters of wrestling. Thank you for sharing your time, knowledge and friendship.

Finally, I wish to express, on behalf of the entire White clan, our gratitude for the hundreds of wrestlers, parents, managers, mat maids and grappler gals whose efforts and accomplishments brightened our lives for nearly four decades. To us, they always were, and will continue to be, family!

Introduction

The persona of the "old coach", eminently successful as a mentor of young men and women but infamous because of his lack of effort in the classroom, is an unfortunate myth. Invariably, great coaches are great teachers because they possess;

- ➢ a consistent, realistic vision of what success looks like.
- ➢ a determination to develop and implement a plan that reflects their vision.
- ➢ an exemplary work ethic that allows their plan to be translated into action.
- ➢ infectious enthusiasm and a passion for teaching that inspires and motivates their athletes.
- ➢ the will to tirelessly promote their program and its participants in the effort to generate community support, build confidence, develop pride and establish a tradition of excellence.
- ➢ an understanding of empowerment's role in promoting leadership development and in accelerating program growth.
- ➢ a willingness to provide positive leadership and to hold themselves, personally and

professionally, to the highest standards of effort, ethics and conduct.

iv

CH 1
Developing a Coaching Philosophy

There are many paths that can lead a coach to success but when he knows what he believes and why he believes it the road to achievement can be traveled more rapidly, with greater confidence and with fewer missteps.

As wrestling coaches, we spend much of our time planning, organizing, communicating, strategizing, motivating our wrestlers and teaching technique. Eventually, however, most of us come to realize that our calling as a coach also imbues us with the responsibility to guide our athletes toward a life of responsible citizenship.

In my case, it was a line in a high school student's poem that first bridged the gap between the weighty responsibility that I felt to guide my wrestlers in a positive direction and wrestling's unique power to produce good men.

In the years since I first read her poem, my admiration for the wisdom and insight that Connie Spies demonstrated when she penned; "It takes a sport like wrestling to make a boy a man"(5) has grown to become gratitude. I will always appreciate the role that Connie's thoughts played in helping me to develop a philosophy that could serve as a guide on my thirty-eight year journey as a high school

1

wrestling coach. Thanks in part to Connie, my basic beliefs about wrestling and coaching have been solidified for a very long time.

The Evolving Nature of a Coaching Philosophy

Indecision, confusion, frustration and disappointment are hallmarks of a wrestling program that operates in the absence of a guiding philosophy. Most coaches understand the importance of establishing realistic goals as they strive to achieve success, but far too many seem unaware of the value that a carefully crafted, comprehensive coaching philosophy can have in providing direction and focus.

During my early years of coaching I was fortunate enough to fall under the influence of Central Washington University Coach Eric Beardsley. Beardsley's coaching, characterized by an exemplary work ethic, amazing interpersonal skills and unquestioned integrity resulted in an enviable record of success on both the high school and collegiate levels.

As successful as Beardsley proved to be in guiding and developing his own wrestling program, it was his willingness to serve as a mentor and role model for hundreds of his former wrestlers and countless other aspiring coaches that cemented his legacy as one of the greatest wrestling coaches in the history of the Pacific Northwest.

Upon accepting my first coaching job in 1968, I attempted to fashion my own program after what I knew of Coach Beardsley's. I placed heavy emphasis upon superior conditioning, aggressive takedowns and leg control and I enshrined the 4-0 match as the ideal performance. Additionally, I insisted upon exemplary sportsmanship and encouraged my wrestlers to represent their community, school and families in a positive manner. As a result of my failure to fully understand the depths of his coaching philosophy, however, my attempt to emulate Beardsley's approach was incomplete. Never-the-less, the ideas I gleaned from his example were still sufficiently powerful to lead my first team to rapid improvement and a modest level of success.

During ensuing seasons, my failure to recognize the importance of developing a comprehensive coaching philosophy of my own left me vulnerable to indecision and loss of focus. As a result, when encountering attractive new ideas or techniques, I often implemented them in what proved to be an ill-considered or precipitous manner. Predictably, this often served to impede rather than accelerate my team's progress.

Maturation as a coach eventually helped me to realize the danger in such an approach and I grew to recognize that hard work and enthusiasm alone were insufficient to develop the kind of wrestling program that I envisioned. As a result, I began the introspective process that I described in the opening of this chapter and that effort led me to the development of a comprehensive philosophy. (Appendix 1)

As I fully applied that philosophy to my coaching I became more capable of communicating a clear vision, of making consistent, value-driven decisions and I was better able to maintain focus in the pursuit of program excellence. Simply stated, developing and embracing a coaching philosophy helped me to become a better coach and leader.

Using Personal Values as a Foundation

Program direction is significantly impacted by coaching decisions related to technique, instruction, conditioning, style and strategy and those areas are often among the first that coaches consider as they begin to develop their coaching philosophies. However, as important as each of those areas may be, it is, in actuality, a coach's personal values and most deeply held beliefs that should form the foundation of his philosophy. By acting as the template for his decision making, it is those values and beliefs that will ultimately produce conviction and provide program direction.

The three basic constructs that form the foundation of my personal coaching philosophy are my beliefs about success, the power of example and the importance of responsible behavior.

A New Definition for Success

About midway through my coaching career I decided to shift the focus in the wrestling program from wins and losses to effort and improvement. Originally, I had implemented the change because I felt that it would stimulate program growth and improve retention but I soon found that my wrestlers were also becoming more coachable, confident and resilient. By focusing on preparation and by enshrining effort as the highest measure of success an environment had been created in which every wrestler could view himself as a "winner" and in which losses could be viewed as opportunities to identify correctable weaknesses. The decision to change focus had created an unintended but important paradigm shift.

The Power of Example

Intentionally or unintentionally, purposefully or unwittingly, coaches exert a powerful influence upon the character development of their athletes.

Growing up in an era when the public expected high school coaches to perform effectively on the field and live exemplary personal lives off it, I had approached my first teaching and coaching assignment with a commitment to do the same. That early decision is one that I have never regretted and, although my effort to serve as a positive role model was at times imperfect, my experiences and observations served to confirm the fact that coaches have a dramatic impact upon their athletes' lives. At no time in life are we more susceptible to the influence of those we esteem than during our teenage years.

When a coach makes and keeps a commitment to serve as a positive role model he strengthens his personal resolve to model ethical behavior, integrity and sportsmanship as he coaches. Sadly, coaches who choose to ignore or abandon that responsibility squander an incredible opportunity.

There are legions of former high school athletes who gratefully acknowledge the positive impact of coaches in their lives. Such individuals are a testament to the power and responsibility imbued in those who coach. Few professions have a greater potential to launch young lives upon the path to positive, personal growth and productive citizenship.

Fostering Responsibility

Athletes learn responsibility when the expectation for responsible behavior is clearly communicated, its value is fully explained, failure to act responsibly is consistently disciplined and responsible acts are encouraged and commended.

The decision to make responsible behavior an area of major emphasis in our program reflected my conviction that, as coaches, we have, implicit in our own responsibilities, the obligation to help our wrestlers grow into good men. I always considered it a "bonus" that the process of helping them become good men also made them better wrestlers.

As a means of encouraging our wrestlers to embrace hard work and responsibility, both as individuals and as a team, we enshrined "blue collar values" as the embodiment of the type of character that we wanted them to develop. The following expectations reflect our characterization of "blue collar values". As athletes and coaches we will:

➢ display commitment by working our hardest every day

➢ conduct ourselves in a manner that reflects positively upon our community, school, families and the wrestling program

➢ earn what we receive by giving "an honest day's effort for a day's wages"

➢ consistently clean up after ourselves, rather than expecting others to do it for us

➢ demonstrate humility in victory, grace in defeat and consistently show sportsmanship in every situation

➢ honor those who support us by conducting ourselves in an exemplary manner and by showing appreciation

Monitoring compliance when embracing an ideology such as "blue collar values" is critical. One daily aspect of our approach that was particularly effective in reinforcing those values was our requirement that all wrestlers participate fully in cleaning the locker room following practices and matches. Those who failed to assist were consistently provided with opportunities to improve their physical fitness so that they would become more inclined to participate responsibly in the future. At times, if the offenders became a bit too intractable, their teammates were also allowed to share in these opportunities for self-improvement. Similarly, when individuals failed to assist with daily mat cleaning, gymnasium preparation, post-match clean-up or various other identified extensions of our "blue collar" work ethic their teammates often shared in the penalty exacted for their indiscretions. In addition to the efforts of the coaching staff to model and monitor our team's compliance, I also empowered our seniors, team captains and select parents to appropriately assist us in the effort. As a result, our wrestlers developed pride in self-sufficiency and soon came to successfully manage those tasks and many others with a high level of efficiency. They also developed a great "esprit de corps" and worked together in a disciplined and spirited manner to complete their assignments.

During my tenure at Clover Park High School I was surprised, but pleased, when a few parents initiated an effort to clean up our portion of the bleachers following an invitational tournament. Aware of our emphasis upon "blue collar values", the parents asked the wrestlers to assist them in the effort and the request was met with immediate cooperation by our entire team. Cleaning the bleachers after events concluded soon became a tradition and, as an unintended consequence, our team and fans were frequently recognized and singled out for praise by our hosts.

It is my sincere belief that when a high school coach fails to devote a significant measure of his time and energy to the teaching of citizenship and responsibility that he has abandoned an inviolable trust.

As coaches we have an incredible opportunity to mold our athletes' development, particularly if we are convinced that their accomplishments, in terms of skill and athletic achievement, pale by comparison to their success in becoming good men. It is the development of their character that will be of greatest consequence to the world as their lives unfold.

CH 2

Program Promotion

During the past forty years the number of athletes participating in high school wrestling in the United States has increased steadily but the growth that has taken place represents the addition of new wrestling programs rather than an increase in team size. (8) In the late 1960's and early 70's coaches had little difficulty filling their wrestling rooms to capacity with aspiring athletes, however, by the time I retired in 2004 wrestling programs with more than thirty or forty athletes were rarities. For wrestling coaches that has been a troubling trend.

Few would argue with the assertion that societal changes have made it progressively more difficult to recruit wrestlers. Some view wrestling as "no fun", too hard" or "too much work" and many who are convinced to turn find that they are incapable of or unwilling to endure wrestling's rigors. Additionally, in many schools and communities wrestling is considered a minor sport, suffering from poor coverage by the media, a lack of fan support and little opportunity for the recognition that is routinely afforded football and basketball players. Consequently, kids often see wrestling as an unattractive alternative to other less demanding activities.

Changing that perception takes hard work and a willingness to promote wrestling in the school and community. In the effort to move his program from obscurity to prominence a coach must identify and creatively employ every possible means of promotion; local media sources, in-school communication opportunities, special trips, celebrations, events and projects, fundraising efforts and support groups to generate excitement about wrestling and to effectively publicize his team's accomplishments.

As improbable as it may seem considering the importance of promotion in the development of a great wrestling program, there are coaches who resist taking on the added responsibility. Some grumble that they "didn't become a coach to run a PR campaign" while others find the thought of adding to their load to be overwhelming. Given the many duties and responsibilities associated with coaching such reactions are understandable but the failure to effectively promote will virtually guarantee a smaller turnout, less excitement about wrestling and slower program growth.

Promotion is hard work but it can also be a rewarding process because once a wrestling become a magnet for aspiring athletes, a source of community pride and the focus of media interest the days of small turnouts, lack of excitement, empty gymnasiums and meager budgets quickly become distant memories. Great wrestling programs do not simply materialize out of thin air and they are not solely produced by exemplary instruction and superior conditioning. Traditions of excellence develop when such ingredients produce achievement and are supplemented by the public recognition and acclaim that effective promotion can fashion. The best advice I can give to aspiring coaches is; "If you want to be the coach of a great program then you must be willing to do all of the things that are required to become a great coach."

Working with the Media

Wrestling rarely receives the attention that is routinely showered upon football and basketball but with creativity and persistence wrestling coaches can open media doors that have long seemed closed to them. Weekly newspapers can be particularly useful in that effort.

As a rule of thumb, when I moved to a new community, I immediately attempted to identify the newspaper that provided the best local coverage of our area and school. It was nearly always a local weekly newspaper. My practice was to make an appointment with the editor and then, during our meeting, to offer to consistently provide program information and results during wrestling season. My proposal wasn't always met with universal enthusiasm but, over time, I found that I could make significant inroads by consistently providing the kind of information that they could use.

Weekly papers, in particular, are eager to fill their pages with news that has appeal for their readership but they are more likely to use such submissions when the provider has granted authorization for its modification. I also found that the probability for publication increased significantly when I made it clear that I did not wish to receive credit as the author of the material I submitted. Establishing credibility also proved to be key and, once I was able to do so, it was always a very short time before my articles were being published as written. With a single exception in one very large urban setting I was always successful in identifying a local paper that would eagerly accept news that was accurately written in a useable format and provided in a timely manner. Once e-mail became available I also found them receptive to receiving digital photos as long as I permitted the paper to decide when and if they wished to use them.

Working with weeklies was definitely a "win-win" situation. By providing articles in which I touted the accomplishments of our wrestlers, quoted my assistants and myself and emphasized the positive aspects of our program I was successful in promoting its growth. By accepting my submissions the paper was, without cost, able to fill space with news of interest and to provide its readers with accurate and complete wrestling coverage.

Developing a mutually beneficial relationship with a daily newspaper can be a bit more challenging for a variety of reasons. Most staff members at a daily paper are specialists, the constituency they serve is larger and it is often more diverse than that served by a weekly. I did discover, however, that the surest way to develop a positive relationship with the sports reporters at a daily paper was to respond quickly, efficiently and accurately to each of their requests for program information. Providing that information in an efficient and timely manner was always appreciated and remembered. Coaches make a huge mistake, however, when they ignore such requests because failing to respond will virtually guarantee that future coverage of their programs will be minimal.

I am aware of wrestling programs that successfully utilized radio and television in their promotional efforts but I was never able to achieve the consistency I desired when working with them. Consequently, I chose to spend my time and energy working with other media sources and when we gained radio or TV coverage I simply considered it an exciting promotional bonus.

15

Some head coaches assume responsibility for communicating with the media themselves. I did so because I enjoyed the process and because I wished to control our message. Others coaches, however, may prefer to assign a mature, competent assistant to perform such duties. Whichever model is adopted it is crucial for program credibility and the development of good media relations that all results be accurate, unbiased and provided in an expeditious manner. In our program we reported all results and consistently called in our losses as well as our wins. That effort often earned the gratitude of the newspaper staff and, over time, fostered better coverage for our program.

The following guidelines are a summary of the procedures I followed to foster a mutually beneficial relationship with the media:

➢ Be consistent in your effort to provide useful information. If you can be counted upon to consistently provide your team's results your submissions will be anticipated and viewed more positively. This will greatly increase the likelihood that the information you provide will show up in print or be broadcast.

➢ Make certain that the material you submit is entirely accurate. It only takes one major error to destroy your credibility. Developing a reputation for accuracy will enhance the potential that your submissions will be used.

➢ Take the time to proof-read and perform spell and grammar checks on your submissions. Those to whom your submissions are directed work in the world of words and they are no more tolerant of illiteracy on the part of coaches than you are of inaccuracy or ignorance on their part when they quote you or write about wrestling.

Mat Maids

Prior to the start of my first season as a coach in 1968, I read an article about the Mat Maid groups that were forming across the country and found the possibilities intriguing. I asked a number of girls in my classes if they would be interested in forming a group and the Warden High Mat Maids Club was born.

The girls quickly became an asset to our program; serving as statisticians, decorating lockers, creating promotional posters, assisting with team fundraisers and generating excitement about wrestling in the school and community. My first experience was so positive and productive that, for the next thirty five years, I continued to organize a Mat Maid group each time I accepted a position as head coach in a new school.

I normally chose to serve as the club advisor to ensure communication and coordination but, in a few instances, I was able to identify an interested staff member who served in that capacity and lifted some of the work load from my shoulders. In each case the Mat Maids did a remarkable job of performing their duties and became powerful advocates for the wrestling program.

Fundraising

Within a few months of becoming head coach at Warden I discovered the amazing power that fundraising could have in unifying a team and community. It was the disclosure that the wrestling mat had been tightly rolled and stored in a dry, dusty storage closet for several years that caused me to embark upon my first fundraising experience. Since the mat was in a terrible state of disrepair, I immediately requested the funds necessary for its replacement. Predictably, my naïve request was rejected. Without other viable options it soon appeared obvious that if we wanted a new mat at Warden, we would have to earn it ourselves.

Four thousand dollars was a lot of money in 1969 but with many hours of effort by the wrestlers and mat maids, and with the support of the community, we had the mat we wanted when our next season began.

My team's enthusiasm and willingness to earn their mat really caught the attention of the community. The decision to avoid soliciting donations, relying instead upon projects that provided goods or services in return for the funds we received, had also generated a great deal of good will and the local weekly, the Warden Register, ran a very positive editorial entitled; "They Work For What They Want". (3) From that point on the wrestling team at Warden became the "apple of the community's collective eye" and our program was on its way!

That initial lesson in fund-raising's power to promote program growth and generate excitement proved to be a lasting one for me. Applying the same model, I successfully utilized fund-raising to promote the wrestling program in each of the communities I coached in over the next four decades.

When giving consideration to fund-raising, it is always prudent to anticipate the potential for discord that a major project can generate within both the wrestling family and the business community. In our effort to avoid those pitfalls we adhered to the following guidelines, particularly when we were earning funds to travel.

➢ Each participant was given the option of earning sufficient funds to pay for the trip or

19

to pay for it out of pocket. Progress was tracked and publicized monthly.

➢ Timelines for accumulating a minimum amount of earnings or contributions were established and those who failed to meet them lost the opportunity to participate, forfeiting their claim to their previous earnings.

➢ We allowed family members to participate in our projects but credited all of their earnings to the team member that they represented.

➢ When raising funds we neither asked for nor accepted cash donations and we avoided competing with local businesses in providing goods or services.

When my team was involved in a large fund-raising projects I consistently found that they enjoyed working together, side by side with their coaches and families, in the effort to achieve a common goal. I also found that the excitement and publicity that our projects generated always attracted a substantial number of new recruits to the wrestling program.

Travel

It took me a few years to recognize the power that a special trip could have in promoting the growth of my wrestling program. Once I had

20

experienced it, however, it was a method that I frequently employed to jump start a new program.

When hired as head coach at Zillah High School in Washington's Yakima Valley I was greeted by a small group of wrestlers and three outstanding assistants. I was also fortunate enough to find that my principal, Ray Cooper, had been a highly successful wrestling coach prior to becoming an administrator. The situation seemed ideal until I discovered that wrestling had historically been treated as a "stepchild" in both the school and community in Zillah. There had been a few bright spots in the wrestling program over the years, particularly during Coach Bob Spain's tenure at the Leopards' helm, but Zillah had never developed into a wrestling power and interest in and support for the program was minimal.

Wrestling's relegation to the realm of "minor sports" in Zillah was further confirmed when I discovered that that my team would have the dubious honour of using the school cafeteria as a practice facility. It was bad enough to have to move the tables, clean the floor and lay-out, disinfect and tape the mats each day, but we also had to return everything to its original position once practice ended. This effectively added thirty minutes to our practice time. I also found that I was expected to end practice a hour early each time we had a home basketball game since the cafeteria became the gymnasium's foyer for those highly favoured events. Both situations clearly pointed to the fact that in Zillah, wrestling was an afterthought.

That impression was further reinforced by the abysmal attendance at our first home match. It was obvious that the wrestling program needed a quick infusion of excitement if we were to attract more athletes, generate community support and accelerate the building process. Recalling a conversation that I had had with Coach Larry Gibson of Omak, I contacted him about the process that he had utilized to travel to Hawaii with his team.

After my conversation with Larry I cobbled together a rough proposal and presented the idea of traveling to a Christmas tournament to our principal. Although skeptical, Ray gave me permission to prepare a more complete proposal that would outline the objectives for the trip, our fund-raising goals and the procedures that we would follow during the effort. When the assignment had been completed I invited my wrestlers and their parents to attend an organizational meeting and we discussed travelling to Hawaii the following season.

With the enthusiastic backing of the parents our proposal was soon approved by the school board and we embarked upon an exciting, year-long effort that culminated in our first trip to Hawaii.

As a direct result of that initial trip the wrestling team came close to doubling in size in a single year and Zillah's interest in wrestling began to blossom. Years later some of the kids who made that trip confided that they had only joined wrestling because they had wanted to go to Hawaii. For me that was a confirmation of the power that a single trip could have to stimulate interest in a struggling program. The quick infusion of excitement that our trip to Hawaii provided had truly altered our course and set us on the fast track to improvement.

Miscellaneous Promotional Tools

Websites, schedule posters, team newsletters and in-school promotional opportunities such as announcements, display cases, highlight videos, scrapbooks and event programs can all be used effectively as promotional tools.

Specifically, with respect to school announcements, it was always my practice to announce all of our results and not just our victories. Coaches that exclusively publicize their successes quickly come to be viewed with scepticism and, eventually, with disdain, by both staff and students. Reporting losses to the media and including them in in-school publicity gives your program credibility, provides a healthy dose of humility for athletes and coaches alike, and serves as a reminder that there is always room for improvement.

Team websites and newsletters can be powerful instruments in the effort to promote a wrestling program but I have learned that for most coaches it is best to delegate the responsibility for them to a motivated assistant or a volunteer parent. Each is a time consuming undertaking and by providing the information, results, and photos to be posted or printed a head coach can guide the process without worrying about issues such as design, publication and distribution. Websites have an additional liability built into them. Unless the information posted is accurate and continually updated in an efficient manner the site can become a liability rather than an asset. An inaccurate or out-dated site will frustrate those who view it and, fairly or unfairly, it will send a negative message about your organizational abilities.

A team schedule poster can also be a valuable promotional tool. Distributing them to sponsors and posting them in other visible locations within the community has a positive impact upon attendance and is a simple means of keeping wrestling in the public eye. There are many companies eager to provide this service but I preferred to develop my own posters and to use the revenue generated by ad sales to directly support the wrestling program.

In-school displays related to wrestling are particularly useful in capturing the attention of students and staff but they must be attractive, colorful and current to attract repeat visitors.

Shortly after arriving at Clover Park High School in 2000 I noted a seldom-used display case in a busy hallway near the school's entrance. After seeking and receiving permission to use the case during the wrestling season I began posting a new display each Monday morning. In just a few weeks, it had become a "magnet" for both students and staff with hundreds viewing it each day. My wrestlers ate up the attention the display generated and I often saw them dragging a friend or teacher down to the case to see their latest photo, point out a recent win, show off their selection as "Wrestler of the Week" or brag about our latest trophy. Incredibly, the display case at Clover Park became one of the busiest spots in the school during the wrestling season and the increased interest that it generated helped attendance at our home events to swell.

I also used a promotional theme and t-shirt in an annual effort to create excitement about the wrestling program. I usually developed the theme in consultation with our team captains and seniors and we always tried to sell the shirts at cost. We viewed them as promotional rather than as a source of revenue and, whenever possible, we gave them to the custodians and building administrators to show our appreciation for their support. To my initial amazement many of them became wrestling fans as a direct result of that simple gesture.

Manufacturing Celebrations

The power that a homecoming can have to inspire stellar performances, capture a community's attention and fill the bleachers is universally recognized and appreciated. It's rare to find a former athlete without a cherished story to tell of a parent's night or traditional rivalry that impelled them to an exceptional effort or achievement. Celebrations and special events create excitement, provide motivation and can elicit great performances but they are a particularly potent promotional tool.

Harnessing our almost universal enjoyment of a party or big event; communities, theme parks and businesses routinely attract crowds of revelers with celebrations. When there is no holiday or special event on the calendar, many have learned that they can manufacture one and achieve the same ends. I have found this same approach to be as equally powerful in generating excitement about wrestling in the school and community.

My wrestling schedule included three or four home duals during a typical season and, eventually,

I turned each into some sort of celebration. Parent's night, favorite staff member night and alumni night were particularly successful but at times we also attracted new fans with senior citizen night, junior high night, family night, community appreciation night and other promotional celebrations. With administrative approval the "featured" fans were admitted free of charge or at a special rate and many first time attendees became regulars following their initial exposure to wrestling.

Favorite staff member night was a particularly successful event. It consistently generated good relations between the wrestlers and the staff and it was always well attended. Invited staff members seldom failed to show up and, after sitting at mat side during their host wrestler's matches, many became devoted wrestling converts.

When several wrestlers expressed a desire to invite the same staff member as their guest we allowed seniors priority. We also encouraged our wrestlers to invite a teacher or administrator with whom their past relationship had been strained or who taught a class in which they were struggling. The results were often quite amazing! In particular we encouraged that invitations be extended to key individuals such as our building principal, athletic director, basketball and football coaches, school nurse, head custodian, office manager, secretary and security guard. In most cases those invitations were accepted with surprise and appreciation, producing a new level of interest, support and even advocacy for the wrestling program.

In several schools I discovered that once they had been invited as favorite staff members that many of our youthful teachers, in particular, became regulars, showing up as a group for our week night duals. Their participation proved to be particularly valuable because they always talked about the match the next day; passing their enthusiasm on to their students, focusing attention on the wrestlers in their classes and promoting a positive image of wrestling.

Starting and ending each wrestling season with a well organized, fast moving celebration virtually guarantees an enthusiastic start and a satisfying conclusion. By bracketing a wrestling season with pre-season and post-season banquets, program goals can be communicated, questions can be answered and motivation provided as each season begins and food, fun and successes can be shared as it concludes. By recognizing outstanding contributions, encouraging involvement and celebrating successes banquets can create the type of "family atmosphere" and excitement that will ensure continued support.

Special Recognition

Promotion can produce advocacy when individuals feel that their efforts have been appreciated and public recognition can be a very effective means of providing it. For the most part, we used our home events and team banquets to recognize those who had shown long term support for the wrestling program. For the selfless individuals so honored, the presentation of a thirty dollar plaque and a sincere expression of gratitude became a deeply moving experience. As powerful as a public presentation can be in producing advocacy, such recognition should always be bestowed because it is the right thing to do rather than because of its power to promote.

Recognizing athletes for their special contributions or efforts can also be an effective means of promotion. We used a Wrestler of the Week recognition program for that purpose, highlighting one or more athletes who had displayed an exemplary attitude, shown great courage or performed at an exceptionally high level in competition. Our most skilled wrestlers were often the recipients of the honor but, at times, we consciously chose to select kids who had shown great desire in a losing effort. This spread the recognition around and it also allowed us to further emphasize our program's focus on effort and improvement. A photo of the wrestler was posted in the school along with a short biography and the reason for his selection. The school bulletin was used to announce the award and we submitted it to the local newspaper also including it in our team newsletter and website when they were available. As a result of our Wrestler of the Week promotion teachers frequently made mention of our wrestlers' accomplishments, congratulating them in class, and students and staff regularly stopped by the display case on Monday mornings to see who had been selected for the honor.

Special Events

A well planned special event can be a significant promotional opportunity because it can be used to celebrate your program's successes, showcase local facilities, stimulate school and community interest and motivate your wrestlers to an inspired performance. Invitational Tournaments are particularly well suited to this purpose but hosting them requires a lot of planning and hard work. A word of caution is also advisable because a poorly planned, inefficiently run or chaotic tournament will actually damage your program's reputation.

Ensuring that a tournament is a quality experience for both competitors and fans requires a substantial commitment and those who conduct the event must be provided with adequate training if they are to be successful. Hosting a first class event is impossible unless sufficient resources have been allocated to support the effort and unless each member of the tournament staff is both competent and comfortable in their assigned role. In general it is best to volunteer as a host only after you have developed a highly trained and experienced tournament staff.

Booster groups can be particularly helpful in the effort to host an invitational or post-season tournament. After a couple of years of hosting a single tournament at Clover Park our Boosters developed enough expertise that they were able to successfully host five tournaments in a single season, providing all of the tournament staff and taking full advantage of the fund-raising opportunities that each event afforded.

An additional and obvious benefit of hosting an Invitational is that the home team has a built in advantage in terms of fan support and enthusiasm. The impact of performing well in front of a home-town crowd can be substantial and is certain to produce an inspired effort.

Three of the most exciting special events that I ever hosted were cultural exchange matches with teams from Japan, Poland and Russia. I hosted all three while I was coaching at Zillah and because

31

each occurred during the wrestling season it was a daunting responsibility. Never-the-less, the matches and cultural activities associated with them pulled large numbers of people into our gymnasium serving to promote wrestling in a very meaningful and rewarding way.

Creativity

Coaches who successfully promote their programs tend to be innovators. Creativity always entails risk but the benefits that can be derived from implementing a new idea, activity or approach can be substantial.

During my second season at Zillah our two team captains approached me with genuine concern about the pitiful attendance at wrestling events. Painfully aware that their fan base consisted almost exclusively of a few family members and friends, they found it embarrassing and distressing that the wrestlers often outnumbered the fans at our home matches. They were particularly frustrated because the team had been working hard and was improving rapidly, and yet, the bleachers continued to remain empty. As they pointed out, we had even won a few invitational titles, the first for Zillah in many years, and yet, fans still chose to stay away.

As I listened I also knew that the fact that the gymnasium was packed beyond capacity for basketball every Friday night was also a factor is our captains' discouragement. Impressed by their sincerity I explained that it would take a while for us to develop a winning tradition at Zillah and that, until we did, they shouldn't set their hopes too high. Then I asked them how many people they had asked to come to their last match. A little surprised by the question, they stammered through their responses. It was obvious that they had never considered promoting their own program and so I told them that if they were really sincere about wanting more people in the bleachers that they would have to be willing to invite them. The next day I sought administrative permission to admit senior citizens and families to our next home dual at a discounted rate and I prepared advertising flyers that could be distributed in the community. When the team arrived at practice I divided them into pairs and sent them out, wearing their warm-ups, to knock on every door in town. Those who were contacted received the flyer and a personal invitation to attend the match and those who failed to respond found a copy in their door jam when they returned home. When the evening of the match arrived, as a result of the team's effort, attendance was substantially higher than it had been for our earlier duals and a few of those who chose to attend their first match that evening became real fans.

33

Over the next several years our fan base expanded as our program prospered and attendance eventually increased to the point where one side of the gymnasium was routinely filled for our home duals. Despite our unprecedented successes, however, basketball was still drawing more than twice as many spectators as the wrestling team was. It seemed improbable that we would ever be able to fill the gymnasium to capacity.

Approaching what proved to be my final season at Zillah, a local reporter asked me if I had any remaining goals to achieve now that our team had won a State Championship. Reflecting upon his question I realized that, other than capturing back to back state titles, the only remaining goal of consequence that still remained unfulfilled was my dream of "packing the house" for a dual meet.

At our preseason banquet I announced that we were designating an important league dual as "pack the house" night that season. A few weeks later, as the night of the match approached, I encouraged our wrestlers and their parents to begin inviting their family, friends and neighbors to attend. Meanwhile I did everything in my power to generate interest in the event and, by way of the media and word of mouth, invited the entire community to help us "pack the house".

When the big night finally arrived excitement had risen to a furious crescendo in the school and community and by the time our team took the floor for their warm-up the gymnasium was jam packed. As long time announcer Del Gere whipped the crowd into a frenzy all who were present knew that they were experiencing something very special. Both sides of the gymnasium were filled to capacity and finally, for the first time ever, there was standing room only for a wrestling match in Zillah!

The evening had ended in victory but our team's success in the competition had simply felt like "frosting on the cake" compared to the sense of accomplishment that we all felt over "packing the house". Best of all our entire community had participated in the effort and what had seemed impossible just ten years earlier had become a reality. In reflection I then realized that it had taken a decade of promotional effort and progress to make the phenomenon that we had witnessed that night possible.

36

CH 3
Recruiting

Despite the steadily declining number of athletes in their wrestling programs coaches will sometimes rationalize their inability or unwillingness to recruit by characterizing it as "begging kids to turn-out". Nothing could be further from the truth! Many kids have absolutely no idea what wrestling is all about and unless coaches provide encouragement and accurate information there is little probability that they will ever be willing to give it a try.

Going the Extra Mile

My family likes to tease me by telling others that "Dad never met a boy that he didn't think should be a wrestler!" Their jab is meant in jest but their observation is accurate because I am convinced that wrestling has the potential to positively impact kids' lives to a degree that is unequaled by any other high school sport or activity. Over the years I have gone to great lengths to recruit kids for my wrestling team. For me recruiting has always been a natural outgrowth of the certainty that their involvement will teach them to be dedicated, disciplined and courageous and that those traits will make their lives more successful and productive. When a coach has a passion for wrestling and a conviction that it can change lives, then it is easy to recruit with enthusiasm, persistence and a sense of humor.

Louie

The wrestling season was just three months away and I still had not been able to convince anyone of appropriate size and temperament that the opportunity to fill a projected open spot in our line-up was an amazing opportunity. Our student body numbered less than two hundred and there were a very limited number of boys who were the size we needed and none of them were the least bit interested in wrestling. Louie fit the bill size-wise and he just happened to be in one of my science classes. He was a ninth grader and a bit of a character but he was small in stature, wiry and cocky and he seemed to be exactly what we needed. The problem was that Louie had absolutely no interest in wrestling. When I first approached him about the possibility of turning out his response was an immediate; "I hate wrestling!"

Unwilling to give up easily, I continued to encourage him to come out for the team. Each day as he entered my classroom I greeted him by asking; "Louie, have you decided to come out for wrestling yet?" His response was always the same, a very emphatic; "I ain't wrestling!"

A few weeks later it was time to order wrestling shoes for the guys on the team. We were a rural community located a substantial distance from any sporting goods suppliers and so it was far less expensive to place a group order. As I was finalizing that shoe order it suddenly seemed "right" that I should include a pair of shoes for Louie.

When he walked into my room the next day I said; "Louie, what size shoes do you wear?" Without thinking, he blurted out his size and then asked me why I wanted to know? I mumbled something about just wanting to know and then asked him once again if he was coming out for wrestling. He gave his usual response.

When the shoes arrived I handed them out to the team and then as the day passed I waited in anticipation for Louie to come to class. As he finally entered my classroom, I held up the shoes I had ordered and said; "Louie, your wrestling shoes came in today." With scarcely a pause to collect his thoughts Louie's reply; "I still ain't wrestling!" dashed any hopes that I had that the shoes would make an immediate difference. From that point on, however, each time Louie entered my classroom I responded by holding up the shoes and greeting him with; "I've got your wrestling shoes Louie!" The other kids in the class seemed to get a kick out of our good natured banter with each other and I continued to tease Louie daily about "his" shoes.

Finally, with only a week remaining before wrestling was to begin, I had really given up on Louie ever coming out for the team. By that time I was just hoping that I could recoup what I had spent for his shoes by selling them to another recruit. Fifteen dollars was a sizeable chunk out of my six hundred dollar a month teaching salary.

When Louie came into my room just a couple of days before the start of the season I once again lifted the shoes and said; "Louie, you forgot to take your shoes again yesterday!" and at that point he reached over, snatched them from my hand and said; "Thanks, maybe I'll give 'em a try." I was absolutely astounded!

Louie's mental toughness, wiry strength and hard work eventually helped him become a state place winner as a senior. In addition my experience with him taught me that patience, positive encouragement, persistence, good humor and special attention can play an important in successful recruiting.

Raymond

It was the second week of the new school year and I was taking all of the ninth grade students in my Pacific Northwest History classes on a field trip to the Columbia Gorge. While there I planned that we would be studying and observing some its the amazing history, geology and ecology. We departed at dawn and about an hour and a half later my students were crowded around a historical display near where the pioneers traversing the Oregon Trail had crossed the Deschutes River. Most were frantically taking notes as I had instructed but then I noticed a small group of boys heading toward the river. I moved quickly to intercept them and as I neared the group I noticed that they were being led, like a flock of geese, by a diminutive leader with sagging jeans and a distinctive strut. It was clear that the boy in the lead had taken charge of the group and when I shouted; "Hey, what are you guys doing?" he turned and, with a bit of a sneer and a lot of attitude, responded; "We aren't doing nuthin' wrong!"

It was too early in the school year to have learned the name of each of the sixty plus students on the trip and so when I reached the group I asked the leader what his name was. Remaining "cool" and with a bit of bravado he puffed up his chest and said; "I'm Raymond." As I extended my arm to shake hands with him he met my hand with an immediate and firm clasp and then I asked; "Where did you learn to walk like that Ray?" Drawing himself up to his full five foot four he raised his chin, looked me in the eye, and said; "What do you mean?" "I can walk like that too." I said, and I proceeded to mimic his strut. Turning to face the

41

boys with a smile on my lips and a chuckle escaping my lungs I saw Ray and his group gave each other knowing looks and small nods of approval and they all began to laugh. I asked them how they liked my walk and Ray's response was a good natured; "Not bad! How did you learn to walk like that?" Seizing the moment I asked Ray if he had ever thought about turning out for wrestling. I told him that he seemed like a pretty tough guy to me and that I was always looking for tough guys to be on my wrestling team.

In November Ray showed up at my pre-season meeting. His first year of wrestling was uneventful but as a sophomore he improved with lightening speed, qualified unexpectedly for State and, incredibly, he upset a heavily favored, top-seeded opponent to win his first state title! Two years later Ray finished his wrestling career as a three time state medalist and won his second state championship.

A coach never knows for sure what will motivate a kid to become a wrestler but finding the right key or taking the proper approach can certainly pay big dividends!

Kids Wrestling

An early exposure to wrestling is a critical element in developing the kind of skilled athletes that can significantly impact a wrestling program.

Each time I moved to an area that lacked a youth program I quickly established one. In areas where the program seemed to be headed in the wrong direction I moved just as quickly to reorganize it.

Finding knowledgeable, mature, committed coaches for a kids program can be difficult. Far too many parents find it impossible to set aside their competitive egos and subjectivity and, as a result, kids programs often become mired in controversy and negativity when parents are allowed to coach. To avoid potential problems we also banned parents from mat side during competition but we were equally quick to call them down if their child was hurt or needed comfort.

Desiring to keep our kids program positive and fun for all involved I chose to train my high school wrestlers as kids coaches. This arrangement allowed me to use my assistants and responsible parents as program supervisors and to ensure that quality instruction and high standards of conduct were the norm. By using my own athletes as coaches I was able to ensure that basic techniques were taught and that they were the same ones that we were using in our junior high and high school programs.

Although I had not initially anticipated it I soon discovered that the wrestlers who signed up to be coaches became instant celebrities in the local

43

elementary schools, As a result, interest in wrestling and participation in our kids program literally exploded when they learned that my wrestlers would be their coaches.

Once I had selected a head coach for each team in our program, I scheduled a training meeting where I outlined their responsibilities and provided them with program guidelines and a schedule for practice and competition. I also gave them the list of techniques that I wanted them to teach and discussed the importance of good sportsmanship and being a positive role model. I cautioned the coaches about placing undue emphasis on winning and told them that the kids needed to be able to play and have fun in every practice. Each head coach was then directed to organize and assemble his own staff by recruiting several assistants from among his teammates. Each year there were a few members of my team who preferred to serve as officials rather than as coaches. Those individuals were trained and served effectively as the referees for all of the competitive events in the program. My role was simply to plan, train and coordinate.

The primary purposes for our kids program were simple. We wanted to expose them to wrestling, teach them a few basic skills, allow them to have some fun and help them learn to enjoy competition in a positive atmosphere. We hoped that by exposing them to wrestling at an early age that they would be more capable of making an informed choice when they moved on to secondary school.

On a designated Saturday registration day we weighed every kid, processed their paperwork and presented a short clinic for the wrestlers and their parents. Later that evening I divided them into teams based upon their weight, size and age and determined the team rosters. On the following Monday the rosters were provided to the head coaches and they were instructed to contact their wrestlers and inform them of their practice times and locations. In communities where we had several elementary schools, our coaches organized their own team and practiced in their own school on mats transported from the high school.

Registration was followed by two weeks of practice on Tuesdays and Thursdays. Each weekday practice was one hour in length and we held a one and one half hour clinic each Saturday. This segment was then followed by two weeks of twice-a-week practice and a series of Saturday dual meets. The final two weeks of our program included twice-a-week practices and a Saturday morning tournament. All of the kids received a medal as a result of their participation in our final tournament and an award was given to the highest scoring team. It was interesting to see that the team award was always far more important to the coaches than it was to the kids!

In a few communities, I stayed long enough to see the kids who had started wrestling in our kids program achieve success in the State Tournament as high school wrestlers. In most cases it was those individuals' knowledge and leadership that led the team to post-season glory.

An unanticipated result of using my wrestlers as coaches and officials was that a large number, including our own sons Glen and Chance, later became wrestling coaches and officials as a result of their early experiences working in the kids program.

Team Projects

High School students are almost universally attracted to success and positive activity. In our effort to earn a wrestling mat at Warden, our projects included a weekly car wash and wax, a Christmas wrap sale, the collection and sale of old batteries and scrap metal from surrounding farms, the sale of ad space on our wrestling schedule posters and, uniquely, with the assistance of local farmers we raised, harvested and sold several acres of dry land wheat.

In addition to earning a new mat our projects welded our kids into a solid team and the excitement and enthusiasm associated with the effort attracted many new recruits. Understandably, those who worked to achieve this goal were proud of their new mat and zealous in their concern for its care and maintenance.

While earning a mat at Warden was a seminal experience in my use of fundraising projects to attract recruits, the projects surrounding the Zillah wrestling team's trips to Hawaii were undoubtedly the most ambitious and successful.

The Zillah Hawaii project began with bi-monthly pizza sales. Teams of kids, parents and coaches were formed and assigned to report to a local pizza parlor early on Saturday mornings. At the parlor they prepared pre-sold pizza orders and delivered them to the purchasers. The generosity of the businessman involved in this project was remarkable and, due to his support, our pizza sales generated thousands of dollars in revenue for our trip.

The special projects that we completed in Warden and Zillah were simply two notable examples of the power that exciting projects can have in attracting kids and garnering community support for wrestling. When fundraising is connected to the effort to achieve a highly desirable and specific outcome participant numbers invariably increase and program growth is always stimulated.

47

Removing Barriers

Wrestling has many positive attributes that can be used to entice reluctant recruits to join it. However, when a coach's efforts to encourage participation are rejected it is often because of fear of the unknown or what the recruit perceives as wrestling's potential to expose them to public ridicule or embarrassment. For many kids the fear of competing in public, losing in competition or wearing a skimpy wrestling singlet is more sufficient justification for declining an invitation to join the wrestling team.

I discovered very early that enthusiasm, a positive approach and accurate information were the keys to successful recruiting but I also learned that I could increase the probability for success if I took the time to listen and to remove the barriers that were preventing recruits from making a commitment. Often it was simply fear of the unknown that kept kids from wrestling and so I tried to provide as much information as I could in response to their concerns.

For those who were reluctant to wrestle because they feared losing in front of their friends and family I simply assured them that they would never be required to wrestle a "real match" until they felt ready to do so. This simple assurance seemed to make a huge difference and many reluctant recruits were willing to give wrestling a try under such conditions.

One of the most common barriers that I encountered had to do with the professed modesty that adolescent boys often used as an excuse for declining my invitation to wrestle. For many professing modesty was simply a smokescreen. Adolescent boys, in particular, find it more acceptable to profess modesty than to admit to a lack of courage and, as a result, it is common to encounter potential recruits who cite wearing a wrestling singlet as a major impediment to their participation. Despite my conviction that these claims of modesty are only rarely factual, I made it a practice to purchase uniforms constructed of the heaviest material available so that I could eliminate modesty, real or imagined, as a barrier to participation.

In a few cases church or family commitments threatened to make participation impossible but I also found that showing flexibility in such situations led to an effort on the part of the athlete and his family to minimize the impact of those obligations.

It is seldom necessary to make accommodations for recruits beyond the first few weeks of practice. By the time competition actually began I normally found that most of those who had

49

expressed reservations about participating had forgotten their apprehensions and were clamoring to wrestle.

Retention

Few things are as discouraging for a coach as the loss of promising newcomers in the initial days of practice. This is particularly true when he has put his heart and soul into the recruiting process. It is easy to become disheartened by early season attrition but it is important for wrestling coaches to remember that the demands placed upon participants in their sport are substantially more challenging than those that many kids have faced before and their discomfort will almost always cause them to evaluate the merits of dropping out. New recruits are particularly vulnerable because they lack the experience, desire or self-discipline that can make persevering a better option than quitting.

Feeling somewhat demoralized by the high percentage of recruits that I was losing each season I recognized a number of years ago that it was time for me to examine my coaching practices. I either needed to stop putting so much effort into recruiting or I had to revise my thinking regarding the composition of our practices. I was getting a lot of kids to turn out but it was obvious that I was losing a lot of them because of the intensity of our early season practices.

In response to that dilemma I decided that I would continue to recruit heavily but that I would shift the emphasis in our early practices from physical conditioning to instruction. That adjustment proved to be successful in terms of retention but there were still kids who quit before Christmas. The greatest challenge associated with the change was that our early season fitness level slipped a bit and that elicited some criticism from parents and fans. By the end of the season, however, our successes had quieted the critics and had confirmed the value of the change.

Wrestling can be an emotionally overwhelming experience for beginners. Few other sports require a participant to expose his lack of strength or skill in as public or potentially humiliating a way as wrestling. I have coached a number of gifted, technically sound and well-conditioned athletes who quit my team solely because they were unable to cope with the stresses associated with competition. Athletes who are consistently disabled by irrational fears and those who are unable to accept defeat with a resolve to do better the next time, seldom survive a full season. For such individuals wrestling can become an overwhelmingly negative experience.

While it is true that wrestling is not for the faint of heart, coaches and experienced wrestlers almost universally recognize that it can be an incredibly growth promoting activity for those who choose to endure. The following cautions, if followed, will help coaches improve their retention numbers:

➢ Avoid pairing inexperienced wrestlers with veterans during early season drilling and competition. Because kids who are new to wrestling are easily discouraged their desire to wrestle can quickly be destroyed if they are treated with impatience or get "beat-up" during the first few days of practice.

➢ Include an opportunity to have some fun in each of your early practices. Use relays, tag-team matches, King of the Mat, War Ball, Pretzel, Crab Soccer, scramble drills and other enjoyable activities to provide a few minutes of "play time" each day. In doing so I was surprised to find that our veterans enjoyed the fun just as much as the new recruits and that practices passed more quickly for everyone.

➢ Don't put young athletes on the front lines before they are truly ready. In many cases the same athletes that I was hesitant to use in varsity competition as ninth and tenth graders played key roles in my team's success as juniors and seniors. Forcing them into a varsity role too early can be destructive.

➢ Be selective about the opponents that you allow young wrestlers to face. There are occasional freshmen and sophomores who possess the maturity and technical skill to compete on equal terms with more mature opponents but it is advisable, particularly with kids who are large for their age, to exercise caution.

➢ Eliminate all "rites of passage" or initiations from your program. Such negative behaviors and traditions can quickly become abusive and their continued existence discourages participation.

The effort to minimize attrition is a valuable endeavor but there is a point where attempting to retain a troubled or disaffected athlete is no longer productive. When that point is reached it is best to allow a kid to quit gracefully. Despite our personal convictions about the value of wrestling, the fact remains that our time and effort can be better spent in working with the kids who display a willingness to grow and mature than in chasing after those who are not.

54

CH 4
Program Building

Building a new program can be a daunting process. It requires a solid plan, fierce determination, consistent effort, complete dedication and a positive outlook. For coaches who are willing to commit to the process I believe that it can be the most exciting and rewarding of coaching experiences.

After stumbling into a career as a wrestling coach I soon discovered, to my surprise, that I had a passion for coaching and that I truly enjoyed the excitement and challenge of program building. As a result, throughout the latter half of my career, I consistently sought jobs in schools with under-achieving or struggling wrestling programs. Invariably, I found that the athletes and parents in those schools, after years of frustration, were hungry for change and that they eagerly celebrated each achievement and positive development on the road to success.

As a young coach I often wondered if I would ever have the ability or the opportunity to elevate a wrestling program from obscurity to a state championship. My first state championship experience did little to answer that question because I inherited a great team when I moved to

Alaska's Chugiak High School in 1973. After the initial flush of excitement at landing the best wrestling job in Alaska faded I soon realized that the previous coach had left the cookie jar at Chugiak half full and that the veterans that were returning would have to be supplemented by new recruits.

Many of the new kids that I recruited came out because they believed that a coaching change might provide them with an opportunity to break into a circle of success that had previously seemed unattainable for them. Wrestling was king at Chugiak and wrestlers occupied an esteemed position in both the school and the community. Most of the new kids were pretty raw and that first season turned out to be a challenging one. Never-the-less, our veterans saw to it that a mediocre season was capped with a state championship.

Winning that state title was an exhilarating experience but I was never really confident that my coaching had played a significant role in my team's accomplishment. In some respects I honestly felt that I had simply been fortunate enough to avoid making the major blunders that could have derailed my team's pursuit of their championship.

It is said that experience is the best teacher and, after twenty-one years as a wrestling coach, Washington's Zillah High School provided me with the opportunity to put my experiences into play. Zillah's wrestling program had seen several coaches come and go in quick succession and had been languishing for years. It was a perfect opportunity to discover if I was actually capable of building a state championship program from the ground up. In my initial season we won an invitational tournament for the first time in recent memory and six years later, when my youngest son was a senior, we placed second in the state tournament. It would be an exhilarating ride but it was to take a total of ten years before we captured our first state title.

The climb to the top at Zillah was a challenging but rewarding experience and, once our state championship was achieved, I was a little surprised to find that I had actually enjoyed the journey more than the attainment of the goal. A fellow coach seemed incredulous when I confirmed during my final season at Zillah that I was interested in moving to a new school. I told him that I wanted one last opportunity to build a program from scratch. He seemed bewildered and his comment; "I can't believe that you would actually consider leaving this program after all the hard work and effort that you and your assistants have put in to building it!" was an honest expression of his amazement. We both knew that my team was well on its way to a second consecutive state title.

I left Zillah the following year after accepting a position as head coach at Clover Park High School in Lakewood, Washington. Clover Park had been a wrestling powerhouse during the nineteen seventies and eighties but, in the years since their glory days, the tradition of wrestling excellence that had once flourished had been all but lost. Participation in wrestling was minimal, expectations were low and the prospects for success were almost universally viewed as dismal. It was just the opportunity that I was looking for!

With tremendous support and a mandate from the school administration to rebuild the wrestling program I was determined to get things rolling as quickly as possible. Before classes began that fall I familiarized myself with the school's storied wrestling history and sought out as many former Clover Park wrestlers and coaches as I could locate. It quickly became apparent that there would be a significant base of support for a rebuilding effort.

Once school started I began the effort to organize a staff that would be willing to embrace a new system and new ideas. Most of the applicants I interviewed lacked the ability to make the kind of commitment that I knew building would require and so, in the end, I selected two individuals with limited wrestling background as my assistants. Bill Wilson and Andy Franco were both men of maturity and character and after spending spent several weeks familiarizing them with the philosophy that would guide our program, instructing them in their areas of responsibility and teaching them the technique series that we would be utilizing I was confident that I had made the correct choice in their selection .

With an eye toward stimulating interest in wrestling I next began to post items of historical interest in the school and to plan the special events that I hoped would attract fans to our matches. I also initiated a campaign to recruit as many athletes as possible to the wrestling program and at our pre-season meeting that Fall over sixty prospects showed up.

It was apparent that the wrestling program would need the support of an organized boosters group to make the kind of progress that I had envisioned. A boosters club existed at CP but the chief interest of those involved was football and I knew that promoting and supporting wrestling would require a more focused effort. At our pre-season banquet that fall I explained our program needs to my wrestlers' parents and asked for volunteers who would be interested in helping form a wrestling support group. We held our initial meeting just two weeks later and began the process of forming our own school-sanctioned, non-profit club. Within two months the CP Wrestling Booster Club, guided by an outstanding president and a full slate of officers, was functioning effectively. Over the course of the next four years I met with our boosters twice each month during the wrestling season and at least monthly during the remainder of the school year. In addition to the thousands of dollars of revenue that they generated in support of wrestling the CP Wrestling Boosters also came to serve effectively as positive ambassadors for the wrestling program.

The explosive growth of the wrestling program at CP allowed us to add two youthful assistants to our staff during our second season and my son Chance and former CP wrestler Ronel Balabat brought additional wrestling expertise and an infusion of energy to our program. By the third season we were attracting up to eighty athletes annually and retaining close to seventy percent of our recruits and the CP Boosters Club was capable of hosting and providing competent staff for multiple invitational and post season tournaments. In 2003 our team captured fifth place in Washington's AAA State Tournament and placed second in the State Dream Duals. In 2004 they won a share of a league wrestling title for the first time in nearly twenty years.

The rise of the Clover Park wrestling program had truly been meteoric but their rapid improvement had been due in equal part to the effort of some great athletes, the devotion of a dedicated coaching staff, the support of a terrific group of parents and the encouragement of an enthusiastic principal. Vision and hard work had played a role but it was the desire on the part of the students, parents and staff at Clover Park that had made the rapid transformation from door mat to respectability possible.

62

CH 5

Creating a Season Plan

A coach with the will to prepare will ultimately find success.

The Value of a Plan

Developing a day-by-day plan for the season as a part of pre-season preparation is a substantial undertaking but it is definitely worth the effort. For years I established season goals, cobbled together a competitive schedule to facilitate my team's progress, worked to develop a schedule of special events that would stimulate interest in the wrestling program and planned a conditioning regimen that I hoped would lead my team to a post-season peak. Despite that effort, I never really considered merging them all together into a single, unified season plan. Finally, after years of struggling to coordinate and independently manage each of those tasks, I decided that it was time to incorporate them into a single document.

I found the initial effort to create a season plan to be extremely challenging and much more time consuming than I had anticipated. In attempting to design my plan so that each practice and activity would contribute to the achievement of the goals that I had established for the season, I was forced to evaluate content and consider placement in terms of the impact that each one would have upon my team's overall progress. Making those decisions proved to be a demanding task but, overall, there was great value in the process because it produced an urgency within me to make each day of the approaching season as efficient and as productive as possible. In the end the season plan that I developed proved to be my first philosophically-sound and fully coordinated approach to a wrestling season. As that season progressed, I also discovered that the plan me better able to assess my team's progress, make needed adjustments at appropriate times and more efficiently move toward the achievement of our goals. I also found that the extensive pre-season preparation that had been required to create the plan actually allowed me to enjoy the season more fully because it had freed me from the burden for extensive daily planning. Having a season plan allowed me to focus my energy on coaching rather than on planning and organization once the season began. It has been said that "the proof of the pudding is in the eating" and, after that first season, I never again coached wrestling without creating a season plan.

As the years passed my plans did become more detailed and effective and, in my final years at Clover Park High School, they encompassed the entire span of time between the pre-season team meeting and our post-season banquet. (Appendix 2)

Developing a Season Plan

As the initial step in putting together a season plan, program and season goals should be established. Those goals will then serve to guide the development process as a schedule of competitive events, practices, team activities and special programs are designed to facilitate their attainment.

Designing a schedule of competition that will be beneficial for your team it of critical importance but it can be challenging to so. League duals and post season tournaments are normally scheduled by prior agreement between entities outside of your control and their impact can substantial. Using them as a starting point, however, the remainder of your schedule should be designed to reflect the experience and ability of your team and to promote the attainment of your season goals. The best schedule for your team will include an appropriate balance between events that offer them the opportunity for success and more demanding experiences that will significantly challenge them. A properly designed schedule will promote growth and stimulate improvement.

It can be tempting for a coach to create a weak schedule that will guarantee a string of successes for his team. A schedule that assures consistent success over inferior opponents can generate a measure of public acclaim but it almost invariably produces unwarranted confidence and retards team and individual progress. A soft schedule can leave wrestlers ill-equipped to cope with adversity and disappointment and will virtually guarantee a post-season collapse. As with many coaching decisions, building an appropriate competitive schedule is a bit of an art. Accurately assessing your wrestlers' ability and potential and reflecting those assessments in your schedule will, however, improve the probability that your team will experience positive growth and achieve meaningful success.

Crafting a productive season plan also requires a careful review of the skills, techniques and strategies to be taught during the season. In my coaching I found that it was valuable to spend a portion of my pre-season time and energy in deciding what "not to teach". By limiting what you teach to essentials that will reinforce your philosophy and produce focus, it is more likely that an instructional sequence and drilling system that will promote mastery can be developed.

The final step in the process of creating an effective season plan is to craft a physical conditioning regimen that will promote the steady, even-paced acquisition of the fitness that is necessary for the achievement of a post-season performance peak. (See Chapters 9 and 10)

Once each of the necessary components has been considered and developed, the process of blending them together into a season plan can be accomplished. In the end a well designed season plan that reflects your program philosophy will serve as a steady guide and will ensure season-long organization, efficiency and focus in the achievement of your goals. (Appendix 2)

68

CH 6

Practices

My generation was raised by parents who were inclined to intone the old adage "practice makes perfect" if we chaffed about the need for repetition in mastering a task. Coaches, on the other hand, need little convincing that efficient, effective practices produce superior performances. The coach who can consistently plan and implement such practices lays a solid foundation upon which his team's success can be built as a season progresses.

Practice Planning

When I purchased a copy of The Mike Milkovich Practice Schedule for High School Wrestling Coaches (2) in 1977 I had never even considered that there might be value in planning an entire season of practices before the season had actually begun. However, reading that Milkovich had led his Maple Heights High School (Ohio) team to an incredible twenty-two top ten finishes, including ten state titles, in twenty-seven years, I knew that I had to take look at his system!

Forty dollars was a fortune for us in 1977 but, with Linda's permission, I sent Milkovich a check and in return received fifty three mimeographed pages that changed my life as a coach. As I reviewed Coach Milkovich's daily schedule of practices I was immediately struck by the fact that the workouts seemed to reflect a subtle but progressive adjustment in intensity as the season progressed. It occurred to me that this might have been one of the keys to his ability to successfully peak his team with such amazing consistency. This idea was a real revelation to me because, at that point in my coaching career, I had always assumed that "more was better" with respect to practice frequency, duration, work load and intensity. Suddenly, it seemed clear that my approach to practice had been the root cause of some my teams' early peaks and frustrating post-season performances. It was a humbling revelation. It also occurred to me that my constant focus on hard work had caused me to miss the mark with respect to the fact that my wrestlers needed an adequate amount of rest and recovery time to do their best and to peak properly.

When considered together, I finally understood why the majority of my wrestlers had seemed to be physically stronger at the start of the season than they were at its conclusion. I had, by insisting upon long, intense, daily work-outs, turned a blind eye to their very real need for time off to enjoy family activities, holidays and other pursuits. I had been pushing them far to hard for far too long and I had harvested exactly what I had sown. It was time to change!

In my initial effort to begin a season with pre-planned practices I first considered applying Coach Milkovich's schedule just as he had written it. It quickly became apparent as I examined it closely, however, that the substantial differences between the wrestling seasons in Ohio and Alaska would require me to modify it so that it would fit our circumstances. The adjustments that I made that first year were imperfect but I did find that using the schedule relieved me of much of the burden for planning daily practices. As a result, I had more time to reflect upon my team's progress, analyze their performances and design and implement practice adjustments that led to improvement. Overall, the benefit derived from that first effort motivated me to once again design a practice schedule for the following season.

After spending a few years tinkering with my practice schedule, I noticed that the adjustments I was making in the composition of practice as the season progressed seemed to reflect the differing needs of three distinct phases of the season. Those segments included; a beginning phase where the emphasis was on instruction, a mid-season phase in which conditioning and technique mastery were the focus and a late-season phase where I was intent upon achieving a peak in terms of skill, fitness and performance. It was that observation that prompted me to formalize the adjustments into three distinct practice modalities.

> **Early season mode**- In this mode the focus is upon technique instruction and the progressive development of physical fitness. Practices are a maximum of two and one half hours in length and once the athletes appear to have developed a solid foundation of technique and fitness they may be shortened somewhat as the transition into mid-season practice mode begins.

> **Mid season mode**- In this mode there is a greater emphasis upon conditioning, drilling and live wrestling. The duration of live wrestling is steadily increased and drills emphasizing chaining and timing are stressed. As practice intensity is increased the total practice volume (time) is further reduced.

> **Late season mode**- In late season mode the intensity of the live wrestling increases significantly but decreases in duration. Emphasis is placed upon "technique polishing" through the use of strict-drill. Fitness is also polished through live wrestling, morning sprints and intense but shorter periods of physical conditioning.

Practices are reduced to approximately an hour and a half in length by the end of the season. Considerable attention is also given to strategic and psychological preparation.

I also designed each practice mode to include two distinctive types of practices; a Full Day Practice and a Study Table Practice. (Appendix 3) With the exception of the instruction-laden initial two weeks of the season, both the early and mid-season practice modes included two Study Table Practices per week.

On study table days our wrestlers were required to shower, dress for practice, clean the mats and then report at the normal practice time to a specific classroom with their study materials in hand. All wrestlers, regardless of their grades, were required to attend study table and homework and reading were the only approved activities. The forty-five minute study period and a five minute transition to the wrestling room were considered to be a part of practice.

Study table proved to be a very successful part of our program and, in addition to improving our kids' grades and providing a valuable change in routine, we often received positive recognition as a result of our effort to emphasize academic progress.

Productive Practices

I am convinced that a properly planned, well organized wrestling practice should be no more than two and a half hours in length. When practices are tightly scripted and efficiently run a great deal can be accomplished in a relatively short period of time. The temptation to extend practice beyond the limits of good judgment is, at times, felt by all coaches but it should be resisted. I have consistently noted when I have allowed practices to become too lengthy that my athletes' ability to focus has become diminished, that the vitality and spirit that can make practice enjoyable is destroyed and that the incidence of injury multiplies dramatically. Athletes cannot help but function less effectively when they are mentally and physically fatigued.

One area that can become a problem for coaches as they attempt to limit practice length is the amount of time that is used to set-up and transition between the various segments of practice. One of the simplest ways to increase efficiency in this area is to develop standardized procedures for making such transitions. Once such procedures become automatic for your team they can be made with efficiency and little time will be lost in the process. One of the values of using a pre-planned schedule of practices is that the wrestlers and the staff become so familiar with the practice segments that the transitions become seamless. An additional problem that can be associated with excessively long practices is that they are sometimes viewed by athletes as an indicator of their coach's lack of appreciation for the other interests or concerns in their lives. While it is reasonable to expect athletes to be present and to give their very best in practice each day, coaches should take care to ensure that practices do not substantially interfere with their wrestlers' ability to study, interact with their families and fulfill their other obligations. A failure to reflect an understanding and appreciation for such concerns will invariably cause performance to suffer and attitudes to slip as the season progresses.

I first became sensitized to this issue when I was in high school because of my coach's penchant for spontaneously extending his practices beyond three hours. Coach rarely, if ever, ended practice at the announced time and that proved to be a remarkably counterproductive tendency because it taught us to "save ourselves" rather than to give our very best throughout practice.

Starting practices on time is just as important as ending them punctually. A coach who is unable to start and end practice on time draws attention to his organizational deficiencies and, by consistently failing to keep his commitments, he weakens his moral authority as a leader. What we do communicates what we believe far more eloquently and powerfully than what we say. Penalizing our wrestlers for tardiness while failing to adhere to our own announced timelines smacks of hypocrisy.

In my own wrestling program I attempted to utilize every moment of practice time as efficiently and effectively as possible and I worked hard to ensure that each activity flowed smoothly and directly into the next. By eliminating time lost in sloppy transitioning it is possible to extract maximum value from each and every practice.

With the exception of an occasional extension of practice because of sloppy drilling or other violations of our practice ethic, I consistently ended practice at the announced time. As a result, my athletes seldom failed to respond to admonitions to "push themselves" or to work hard enough to "extend their personal quitting point". Knowing exactly when practice will end serves to motivate athletes to consistently give their best effort.

Starting Time

Establishing a realistic starting time for practice is a critical decision. The end of the school day is an important time for kids to seek assistance from teachers, socialize with their friends, take care of personal needs or walk their girl friends to the parking lot. Establishing a practice starting time that disallows or makes such activities difficult virtually guarantees that practice tardiness will become a problem.

Prior to the start of each new season I normally asked our captains and seniors to provide input on our practice starting time. It was a good way to demonstrate confidence in their judgment and, invariably, they responded with a suggestion that illustrated their maturity. Thirty minutes was usually deemed long enough to take care of personal matters of importance, dress for practice and clean the mats. As skin diseases became a more widespread problem I began to require every wrestler to shower and to have his skin inspected prior to practice. I added ten more minutes to the span between the end of school and our practice starting time to accommodate this adjustment.

Because our entire team was required to participate in cleaning the mats prior to the start of practice each day, I assigned our captains the responsibility to see that they consistently and efficiently accomplished it. I also designated one of my assistants to monitor and supervise the process and to see that the team warm-up and stretching period began at the designated starting time each day.

A team manager was appointed to record the names and arrival times of wrestlers who failed to assist with mat cleaning or who arrived after the start of practice. Athletes who were tardy were required, on a minute for minute basis, to do extra grass drills once practice had ended. Since we did most of our conditioning during the final twenty minutes of practice each day this penalty was a significant deterrent.

Challenge Matches

Challenge matches were an important part of our practice each week but because we wanted fitness level to play an important role in the outcome of our challenges, we usually scheduled them for the end of practice following our twenty minutes of conditioning. Occasionally, a challenge participant would express concern that they were too tired to do their best in their match because of the demands that conditioning had placed upon them. My consistent response was that our challenge procedures were intentionally designed to give those who were in the best condition the advantage. That always seemed to end the discussion.

From both an athlete's and a coach's point of view, one of the distinct advantages of wrestling is that team positions are earned through direct competition. As a result, accusations of favoritism, often a source of discord in sports like football and basketball, seldom crop up in wrestling. I also found that it was best to use assistant coaches and select seniors as the officials for our challenge matches and I reserved the right to take corrective action when I observed an error in judgment or a misapplication of the rules. A challenger was required to win two out of three matches before he earned the right to replace his teammate in our lineup. A varsity athlete retained his position if he won the first challenge match or, having lost the first match, if he won the next two.

Before I adopted a two out of three policy, a single challenge victory was all that was required for a challenger to earn a varsity position. That procedure seemed to work pretty well until in one snake-bitten season a quick pin produced a major upset in a challenge during the week of a crucial dual. Despite my strong misgivings about the outcome of the challenge I felt honor bound to uphold the result. When the dual was contested and the challenge victor was quickly dispatched by an opponent that his teammate had dominated in several previous outings I knew that it was time for a new challenge procedure.

Despite my preference for the objectivity of challenge matches, other similar experiences convinced me that a head coach needs to reserve the right to make a line-up change when he has subjectively determined that making that change has the potential to benefit the team. Although I rarely replaced a challenge match winner in our line-up, I did make two important accommodations when I felt that such a substitution was necessary. The displaced wrestler was awarded the number of letter points that he would have earned if had he wrestled and scored a pin in the match and he was also provided with the opportunity to wrestle on the varsity level during our next outing.

CH 7

Technique

When I was first hired as a head coach in 1968 the sum total of my wrestling experience was four years, two seasons as a high school wrestler and two college wrestling classes. It was obvious that my learning curve was going to have to be a steep one if I was going to find success as a coach.

Painfully aware of my deficiencies in the area of technique I immediately began to purchase and read every wrestling book that I could lay my hands on and I enrolled in Eric Beardsley's wrestling coaching class at Central Washington University. That summer term class proved to be so valuable that I resolved that I would attend every class, camp and clinic that our meager budget would allow in my effort to become a more knowledgeable coach. The knowledge that I accumulated that summer formed the basis for the instruction that I provided when I began coaching for the first time that November and my commitment to becoming more educated about wrestling continued to pay dividends throughout my career.

As I began that first season at Warden I was particularly careful to note the techniques that were utilized by our competitors. Eastern Washington was virtually loaded with great coaches and

81

powerful programs during the late 60's and early 70's and they proved to be a rich source of information. By my third season, however, as a result of the volume and diversity of wrestling technique to which I had been exposed, I felt like I was drowning in a virtual ocean of information. I was so overwhelmed by the mountain of information that I had accumulated that I lost the ability to provide program clarity and direction. I knew that I had to start making decisions about what I would and would not teach and I finally realized that I needed to filter all technique through the template of my wrestling philosophy. In doing so I was finally able to eliminate those techniques and strategies that failed to fit comfortably within that framework. It was a time consuming and challenging process but, as a result, I was able to re-establish focus and provide the direction my team needed.

Positioning

As the years unfolded I continued to adjust various aspects of my wrestling philosophy and to make incremental changes in the techniques that my teams utilized. It was, however, a presentation on positioning by Moses Lake High School Coach Ron Seibel (4) that most dramatically altered my instructional approach.

The success of Seibel's Moses Lake program, unparalleled in Washington's wrestling history, provided a degree of credibility that I found irresistible. In Seibel's view, position always trumps technique and, as I listened to his presentation, the logic of his reasoning resonated powerfully with my own observations.

I applied Coach Seibel's positioning philosophy to my program by establishing the maintenance of good position as foundational to both our offense and our defense. Once my wrestlers began to understand the value of holding good position while they wrestled, it became apparent to them that recognizing and capitalizing on the positioning errors of their opponents could also be a valuable tool.

Emphasizing positioning rather than technique was a major shift in approach for me and it was accompanied by a dramatic improvement in my team's success. The positioning elements that I emphasized were as follows:

- ➢ On the bottom we will keep our weight back on our legs and feet and off of our hands. We will keep our heads up, our elbows in, our back curved up and our body coiled. We will focus on hand-fighting and attempt to control our opponent's fingers.
- ➢ On the top we will keep our weight off our knees, support ourselves on our toes and force our opponents to carry our weight. We

will place emphasis upon wrist rides, leg control and through-the-crotch rides as we work to control our opponents. Once we have them under control, we will attack our opponents' supporting points, force them out of position and then apply a pinning combination. Unless we are applying a pinning combination, we will stay behind our opponents' elbows.

➢ On our feet we will keep our legs shoulder-width apart, knees and waist bent, weight on the balls of our feet, our elbows in and our heads up. We will carry our hands low and keep them relaxed and we will take care to avoid establishing predictable patterns as we move. We will shuffle our feet to avoid crossing them and we will attempt to create an angle on an opponent before we penetrate.

Teaching Techniques in Series

Techniques that are taught in isolation from each other can be challenging to learn and difficult to recall in competition. By teaching each technique as a part of a series of related skills both acquisition and effective use can be dramatically enhanced.

I was first prompted to begin teaching techniques in series after observing that some of my wrestlers' performances resembled a jumble of car parts rather than the smoothly operating vehicle that I had envisioned when I was instructing them. It was a highly beneficial change. By presenting everything in series my wrestlers learned more quickly, their retention improved and they became far more likely to string techniques together into chains of moves when they were wrestling.

When I am teaching a series I begin by presenting a basic technique and then I progress to the "what ifs" that could occur in a match once the technique has been initiated. Once my wrestlers begin to understand the concept of "action and reaction" in wrestling, the techniques they have learned and drilled in series become automatically associated with particular reactions or situations. At that point the technique really begins to make sense both intellectually and kinesthetically and, as a result, wrestlers begin to develop the ability to wrestle by "feel". Teaching and drilling techniques in series facilitates the development of a smooth flowing, continuous style of wrestling characterized by automatic responses and skilled situational adjustments.

Sticking to Basics

From a technical standpoint there are many approaches to wrestling that can be successful. That being said, placing primary emphasis upon instruction in, and mastery of, high-percentage techniques is one of the surest and quickest ways to achieve success.

All high-percentage moves have two common elements; they can be executed with a high probability of success and when unsuccessful, they seldom place a wrestler in a position of great disadvantage.

Basic skills are, invariably, the technical mainstays of great wrestling programs. As such, they form a solid foundation upon which more advanced and specialized techniques can be added. They can, however, also be utilized by less experienced coaches and athletes to maximize success and to avoid the pitfalls of "big move" wrestling. Upper-body throws and other high risk techniques that are frequently referred to as "big moves" can be used with great success but they usually require an extraordinary degree of skill or athleticism for proper execution. More importantly, a failed "big move" usually results in disaster.

I avoided "big move" wrestling as a young coach because I knew, intuitively, that sticking to basics would keep my wrestlers out of trouble. It was a simple but effective approach and one that produced a modest level of success for my team in a relatively short period of time.

Big Moves

Although I had discouraged the use of throws and other "big moves" early in my coaching career, as I matured I began to recognize that there were certain individuals and teams that could use them effectively. Additionally, I discovered that providing instruction in their use helped my wrestlers to become more effective at countering them.. What proved surprising to me, however, was that my wrestlers seemed to enjoy the novelty of practicing a "big move" and that the introduction of a throw or "clinic move" always made practice more exciting for them. Never-the-less, I continued to emphasize that for most wrestlers and teams, throws and other high risk techniques were to be used only as moves of desperation.

My 1999-2000 state championship squad at Zillah High School was a notable exception. During that memorable season our wrestlers pinned over two hundred and fifty opponents and more than fifty percent of those falls came by way of the head and arm! The kids on that particular Zillah squad just happened to be very, very good with it and had picked the head-and-arm up while participating in youth wrestling. Fortunately, by that time they reached high school I had become a bit more pragmatic in my approach to coaching and when I saw what they were capable of doing with it, I

87

embraced it's use. I also responded to their preference for using the head-and-arm by tweaking my philosophy a bit and working on set-ups and finishes that increased its effectiveness. Predictably, when I left Zillah I returned to my focus on high percentage techniques and I never again coached a team to use the head and arm as a primary weapon.

Promoting Diversity of Style

After several years of insisting that my entire team master and employ my vision of the "correct" style of wrestling, I began to recognize that there were upsides to coaching a team with a diversity of wrestling styles. When wrestlers are encouraged to fully develop their personal gifts and preferences and are provided with the guidance and assistance that they need in doing so, it not only increases each individual's potential for success but greatly magnifies the difficulty of preparing for competition with them.

Once I began encouraging my wrestlers to develop their own distinctive styles some came to rely heavily upon techniques that I had generally discouraged. At Clover Park High School two of my most successful wrestlers developed a preference for a lateral drop. Both had superior strength and back flexibility and, for large men, unusual quickness in their hips. Each also had the confidence required to fully commit to their throw and, as a result, they experienced a high level of success. In both instances, by seeking the assistance of volunteers who possessed expertise in upper-body technique, we provided them with the assistance they needed to maximize the effectiveness of their throws.

During the latter stages of my career volunteers played an important role in my team's success and I came to readily welcome those who were willing to work within the parameters that I established and accept direction. I had come to recognize that while there could be only one head coach, we could never have too many good coaches in the practice room. That decision made it possible for me to encourage and empower volunteer coaches and to pragmatically embrace the knowledge that each of them brought to our program. This approach also contributed to the development of a wide diversity of wrestling styles by my team. I was particularly supportive of volunteers who were willing to work individually with our wrestlers and I encouraged our kids to learn as much as possible from them.

Over time, my willingness to allow mature volunteers to participate in our program proved to be of great benefit and further reinforced my belief that there is no one way to achieve success in wrestling. By making it clear that each wrestler was free to discover his own talents and preferences and by encouraging the development of unorthodox or distinctive wrestling styles, we were able to gain advantage over many of our opponents. To further reinforce that approach I also built a "favorite move" component into our strict-drill routine, giving our wrestlers the daily opportunity to drill their preferred techniques.

The Power of the Pin

I believe that the best defense in wrestling is an aggressive offense. At some point, however, even the most aggressive wrestlers are attacked by their opponents and so it is essential that coaches teach defensive techniques. Never-the-less, I have always chosen to place heaviest emphasis upon scoring quickly and often.

I had been stressing pinning for several seasons before I coached with Steve Wolfe at Alaska's Homer High School but exposure to Wolfe's philosophy influenced me to move even further toward the offensive side of wrestling. In his Five-Point Philosophy (8) Coach Wolfe proposed that every technique should eventually flow into a pinning combination. Wolfe's reasoning that wrestlers who score five point moves usually win their matches and that those who pin their opponents always do, is simple but powerful.

Coaching at Homer I also gained a greater appreciation for the pin's power to electrify fans, provide motivation and produce upsets. Putting some of the elements of Wolfe's philosophy into action I began to place greater emphasis upon teaching and drilling technique sequences that led to pinning combinations. It was an approach that paid significant dividends over the final fifteen years of my career.

Circular Instruction

Preparing wrestlers technically for the first competition of the season can be a challenging task. Typically, competition begins in the third week and it is virtually impossible to provide the necessary instruction and develop technique mastery in such a short span of time. As a result, coaches often press unreasonably to "get everything in" before their first match and, predictably, they end up frustrated because of the impossibility of the task.

My approach to this problem was to employ a method that I referred to as circular instruction. Rather than attempting to have my team master each technique series when it was first presented my practice was to quickly move on to other series without concern for mastery. As a result I was able to present a large amount of technique in a very short span of time. Eventually, by returning to each series a number of times and by drilling it with regularity, mastery will be achieved.

In my first year as head coach at Zillah I was blessed with two young assistants who possessed considerable technical expertise. John Mitchell and Daniel Robillard were both teachers in the district and had been accomplished, highly successful high school wrestlers. They were committed, enthusiastic and capable and the preparation for our first season together went well. However, once practice actually began it only took a few days to recognize that Daniel and John were becoming increasingly uncomfortable with my approach to instruction. Despite the fact that I had taught them the basic technique series that we would be using and explained that my instructional methods might seem somewhat non-traditional, it soon became evident that it would be necessary to do more than simply offer assurances that my instructional methods would be effective.

Near the end of the second week of practice Daniel and John approached me in the locker room office and expressed joint concern. They were worried that I had been spending too much time indoctrinating the kids into my philosophy and they were alarmed by the amount of technique that I had been teaching and by the rapidity with which I had been presenting it. They were certain that our

92

wrestlers would be ill-prepared for competition and that a poor start would jeopardize our chances for a successful season.

After listening to their concerns I reassured them that their questions about my methodology were understandable. Then I explained that it was early in the season and that I was not particularly worried about our conditioning or our level of technical mastery. I agreed that it was entirely possible that we would experience some early season set-backs but reminded them that I would be returning to each series several more times before I had finished instructing our kids. I encouraged them to be patient and to judge my approach by the results that we achieved at the end of the season. As the meeting concluded it was obvious that Daniel and John felt that we were headed for disaster but, to their credit, they listened and remained flexible.

As the season unfolded I returned several more times to each series for additional instruction and supplemented it with extensive strict-drilling. Soon the situation resolved itself and our team began to experience an unprecedented level of success. At the end of the season we qualified twice as many wrestlers for the state tournament as in any season in recent memory.

94

CH 8

Drilling

Drilling is essential to technical development and it is the one common component of every great wrestling program that I have ever observed. For drill to be most effective, however, I believe that it must reflect not only the purpose for which it has been designed but the personality and wrestling philosophy of the coach who implements it.

I started developing the unique drilling style that I refer to as "strict-drill" very early in my career. I wanted my team's drilling to embody elements of repetition, discipline and conditioning and I wanted them to drill with maximum effort, speed and precision on a consistent basis. I had quickly learned that when I instructed my wrestlers to execute five repetitions of a particular move and then allowed them to drill on their own, that many did so with minimal effort and sloppy execution. I had also noted that their wrestling mirrored their drilling.

To rectify the situation I determined that I would develop a drilling style that would demand flawless execution, maximum effort and total concentration from every wrestler. I also wanted to conduct the drill in such a way that I could monitor each member of my team at the same time. It seemed clear that the only possible way to accomplish those objectives would be to strictly control the action during drill and to require simultaneous execution by every member of the team. That was the beginning of "strict-drill".

If any one aspect of my coaching was distinctive it was strict-drill. I used many other types of drilling to provide emphasis and to allow my wrestlers to practice a variety of skills but strict-drill was the drilling mainstay of my program. During strict-drill no athlete was permitted to speak and assistant coaches were assigned to observe and make note of deficiencies but they were not allowed to disrupt the drill itself or provide instruction. To reinforce that policy I always described strict-drill to my athletes and to my assistants as a time to "perform" and not a time to "learn".

Since all team members were required to simultaneously execute each move during strict-drill the procedure involved the announcement of a specific technique followed immediately by a signal to initiate action. As team members performed the technique with maximum speed and efficiency a second whistle signal was used to indicate their return to the ready position. Other than directions from and comments by the coach, absolutely no verbalization was permitted during strict-drill.

Normally, each partner was given three opportunities to execute each technique during strict-drill and, if the majority of the team executed the technique properly, we immediately moved on to the next technique. If execution was sloppy or if there was talking anywhere in the room, the same technique was then repeated until all of the criteria had been met.

Since very little time was allowed for recovery into the ready position strict-drill also served as a tremendous conditioner. As a result, after a just a few weeks our wrestlers were consistently able to drill in a choreographed manner for up to thirty minutes without a word being spoken or a single drilling pair being out of sync with their teammates. Of all the drilling systems that I have ever observed strict-drill best promotes the development of the muscle and nerve pathways that are necessary for techniques to become automatic and effective. During a strict-drill session the brief time between whistles is the only opportunity that a drilling pair has to rest. This intentional design encourages speedy execution followed by a rapid recovery back into ready position. An additional but related benefit of strict-drill is that the pressure to perform immediately upon command improves a wrestler's ability to react automatically to changes in position or situation during competition.

We drilled daily for from twenty to thirty minutes and during a typical strict-drill period I attempted to move my entire squad, in unison, through each of our technique series. (Appendix 4)

Strict-drill is an incredibly demanding activity but it is a very effective means of developing technical proficiency and self discipline. Monitoring performance is, however, critical to its success and the coach directing strict-drill must maintain a watchful eye and develop the ability to see individual lapses as well as team deficiencies as the drill proceeds. To effectively conduct a strict-drill session a coach must also possess a sense of timing and a complete understanding of the techniques to be drilled.

The wrestlers involved in strict-drill must be taught to be good partners and to provide just enough resistance to make the drill effective without disrupting their partner's ability to properly execute each technique. Once they understood the process and the benefits associated with strict-drill our wrestlers always took great pride in the speed and precision of their drilling. They were intolerant of lazy, inattentive or undisciplined teammates and their intense effort to achieve perfection as individuals and as a team virtually eliminated any need on our part to deal with those issues. They also learned that they had to be in top physical condition to have any hope of successfully completing thirty minutes of flawless strict-drill and they came to value it as a highly favored conditioner and method of weight control.

On one occasion, after my team had completed a particularly impressive strict-drill session, a fellow coach approached me and complimented me on my team's performance. Then he asked if I had any idea what the impact of watching my team had been on his wrestlers? He said that it had scared them to death because they could not even conceive of the discipline that would be required to do what they had just witnessed! At times other coaches and wrestlers described our performance during strict-drill as "mesmerizing", "awe-inspiring" or even "intimidating". Some likened our strict-drill to a highly choreographed ballet and opposing wrestlers often revealed that they were overawed by the discipline required for a team to move through thirty minutes of drill without a rest period and without a single sound being uttered. Once I made my wrestlers aware of this phenomenon they began to take even greater pride in the process and we intentionally drilled in front of our opponents whenever possible.

Although the specific techniques that we drilled and the names that I used for them are not particularly important, the strict-drill list that I used during the 2003-2004 season can be found in Appendix 4. By mid-season my team was normally able to complete between fifty and seventy-five percent of the list in a single thirty minute drilling period. The following day we simply started drilling where the previous day's drill had ended.

I frequently utilized a brief team warm-up period and a strict-drill session as our entire practice on the days prior to matches or tournaments. It was a great way to shed a few pounds and our wrestlers looked forward to it because they knew that if they performed effectively and efficiently that practice, while intense, would be short.

As a final note it is imperative that coaches understand that if they choose to attempt strict-drill with their team that they must resist the natural temptation to offer technique instruction during the drill period. Attempting to provide instruction during strict-drill slows the entire process, disrupts the flow and minimizes the benefit that non-stop action can eventually produce. Over the years I had a few assistants who simply "could not stand" to see kids perform a technique improperly during strict-drill. In deference to their personal need to take immediate corrective action, I allowed them to quickly and quietly remove the offending set of drill partners and take them to another area for instruction. When they were finished they quietly reinserted them back into the drill.

In later years I made an additional adjustment that proved to increase the efficiency and value of our early season strict-drill. I made it clear to our inexperienced wrestlers that if they did not recognize a technique when it was announced that they had permission to quietly watch rather than attempt to execute it. As the season progressed, however, I was progressively less tolerant of such lapses and, as a result, by mid- season everyone was usually drilling effectively.

102

CH 9

Conditioning

There are many factors including attitude, technical ability, work ethic, mental toughness and experience that play a significant role in achieving success in wrestling but none are as foundational as physical conditioning.

The value of physical conditioning was first confirmed for me when I was a high school wrestler. Ours was a new program and while our coach didn't know much about wrestling, he did understand the value of being in great shape. Despite our lack of technical ability we won a lot of matches simply because we were able to wrestle hard for a full six minutes, beating superior opponents because they tired more quickly than we did.

My primary goal as a coach, with respect to conditioning, has been to ensure that my wrestlers could compete in a standard six minute match and an overtime without being disabled by fatigue. With that goal in mind I have employed live wrestling and other challenging activities that duplicate the movements and intensity of wrestling as the preferred conditioners for my teams. The logic of using wrestling to condition wrestlers, swimming to condition swimmers and gymnastics to condition gymnasts has always appealed to me and best explains why, unlike many wrestling coaches, I have avoided using running as a conditioner.

Grass-Drills

Grass-drills are one of the few carry-overs from my days as a high school wrestler that I incorporated into my own wrestling program. Other than live wrestling, grass-drills have been the staple in my storehouse of conditioning activities for forty years. During grass-drills a wrestler runs in place and, on command, drops to his stomach on the mat. Upon hitting the mat he immediately bounces back up to his feet and resumes running in place.

In designing my practice schedule I chose to include five minutes of grass-drills in the first practice of the season. The drop rate was a relatively slow pace of one drop every five seconds. In succeeding practices one additional minute was added each day until the grass-drill period was fifteen minutes in length. At that point the period was reduced to ten minutes and the drop rate was adjusted to one drop every four seconds. One minute per practice was again added until the period was twenty minutes in length. At that point the period was once again reduced to fifteen minutes and the drop rate was increased to one drop every three seconds. That rate was then maintained and one minute per day was added until the period length was once again twenty minutes.

Twenty minutes of three second drops is an incredibly demanding pace and, through trial and error, I discovered that a wrestler who could endure it could also wrestle a nine minute match without being disabled by fatigue. Once we reached our twenty minute, three second drop target we maintained that level of effort on a daily basis throughout the majority of the season.

When my team was able to cope with three second drops with comparative ease I added a variety of other elements to our grass-drills. At times we started the grass-drill period with our two lightest wrestlers in the center of the mat and, with their teammates performing grass drills on the perimeter, they wrestled for a takedown. When a takedown was scored the winning wrestler remained in the center and was joined in the circle by the next heavier member of the team. This continued for the entire twenty minutes. My team enjoyed the competition afforded by this variation and the distraction it provided always seemed to make the twenty minutes pass more quickly for them.

In a second effort to introduce variety, I occasionally lined our wrestlers up on one edge of the mat and, at unpredictable intervals during their drops, I would shout; "You're off", to simulate an official's out of bounds call. Responding to the call they were to pop to their feet, sprint to the opposite edge of the mat, bounce on their toes when they arrived and display their "over-time" smiles. I presented this version as an opportunity for them to learn how to "act fresh", "psych-out" their opponent and rehearse hustling to impress the official even though they felt threatened by exhaustion. It was a demanding but effective drill and, although my wrestlers found it supremely challenging, they always seemed to enjoy the change of pace.

It may also be of value to note that I insisted that our wrestlers stay alert, keep their heads up and maintain facial composure during grass-drills. It is extremely challenging to do grass-drills without showing the strain of the activity in your face but our kids always seemed to get a kick out of my insistence that they demonstrate their "overtime smiles" when we neared the end of the grass-drill period.

Executed properly, grass-drills are a grueling exercise and wrestlers will occasionally struggle to maintain the required pace for the full thirty minutes. It was a tradition on our team for their teammates and coaches to exhort them to give extra effort during such moments. Frequently, our senior leaders and team captains moved alongside such individuals providing pacing and encouragement.

We called this "helping" and it fostered the development of leadership, pride and extra effort by everyone.

We also used grass-drills as a means of encouraging our wrestlers to "work like they were a machine" rather than a normal human being, We urged them to refuse to show weakness and to beat their opponents mentally by making them quit first. Invariably, our team whole-heartedly endorsed this philosophy and grass-drills provided a daily opportunity for them to practice and demonstrate their commitment to it.

Each year as we neared the post season many of our more motivated kids would ask if they could do double drops during the final two or three minutes of grass-drills. Their extra effort was encouraged and I praised those who participated for being willing to work beyond normal limits to extend their personal quitting points. This positive development always proved to be infectious and soon most of our team had joined in the effort.

During the latter portion of my career my wrestlers also used grass-drills as their preferred warm-up exercise prior to competition. Our insistence that they "break a sweat" before stepping on the mat motivated them to do their drops wherever they could, even using the bare floor when no other space was available.

At the surprise retirement party my wife Linda had planned at the end of my coaching career it was amusing to find that the question most frequently posed by the wrestlers of one era or school to those of another was; "Did coach make you guys do grass-drills too?" The affirmative response always produced smiles and provided them with common ground that stretched from 1968 to 2004.

Late Season Sprints

Although I was slow to embrace running as a means of conditioning, I began to reevaluate my stance after seeing sprints used as an effective late-season conditioner in another coach's program. I decided that sprints might provide an added boost in my effort to polish my wrestlers' conditioning for our annual post-season push. When I attempted to find a time to run sprints, however, it became apparent that the gymnasium at Zillah was tied-up until late in the evening with a sequence of boys' and girls' basketball practices. As I scrambled to find an alternative it became clear that our only option would be to run the sprints in the morning before school started.

My announcement that we would be running sprints at six in the morning was met, as might be imagined, with a less than enthusiastic response by both my team and my assistants. In lieu of going to battle over the issue I decided to make participation optional but announced that those who attended morning sprints would be excused from the twenty minute grass-drill period scheduled at the end of each day's practice. I also made it clear that I believed that those who were sincere about qualifying for the state tournament would find a way to be present for sprints.

Predictably, the initial response to my announcement was muted and participation numbers were low but when almost overnight, those who were running sprints surged ahead of their teammates in stamina and enthusiasm it became obvious that something good was happening. Twenty minutes of morning conditioning was having a far greater impact than doing an equal amount of conditioning at the end of practice. It was as if some sort of unanticipated physical synergy was taking place. The results were so unexpected and so dramatic that I resolved to install morning sprints as an integral part of my late season practice mode during future seasons.

While several of my teams had enjoyed success in the post-season prior to my implementation of morning sprints, my ability to "peak" my team had been somewhat inconsistent. However, once morning sprints became a standard and required part of the program the consistency with which our peak coincided with the post-season became the hallmark of our team, both admired and duly noted by our competitors.

Eventually, my wrestlers came to take great pride in participating in early morning sprints and were confident that their dedication and extra effort would give them a substantial edge over their opponents as they sought to qualify for the state tournament.

Live wrestling

No other activity prepares a wrestler for competition as effectively as live wrestling. With that certainty in mind I have always included as much live action as seemed advisable when planning practices. However, I learned to be careful during the early part of the season and to tightly control the positions, duration and total amount of live wrestling that I allowed. Painful experience had illustrated that there was a high potential for injury associated with live action during the early season. I was also cautious in my use of live action when I had an inexperienced team. Kids new to wrestling often move in inexplicable and unexpected ways and they can often injure a partner or suffer personal injury as a result. Similarly, when my team had experienced a rash of injuries I usually curtailed the volume of live wrestling or shifted away from full combat to more controlled action emphasizing specific positions or techniques. Rather than going full-out on our feet, for example, I would place our wrestlers in a takedown position or on the mat in a pinning combination and instruct them to wrestle for a pin. In such situations the duration of action was short and, if there was a reversal or escape, the combatants were instructed to stop. This effectively limited my wrestlers' exposure to injury but still gave them the feel of live action.

Using live wrestling to prepare athletes for competition requires a solid understanding of the relationship between intensity and volume. In early season practice mode (Appendix 3) I kept the live wrestling short in duration and moderate in intensity. Injury was a primary concern but I was also aware that inexperienced wrestlers commonly became discouraged if the competition in the practice room became too intense before they were physically, emotionally and technically prepared for it. Discouragement quickly leads to disillusionment and disillusioned kids often decide to quit.

In the effort to minimize losses due to injury and attrition I normally designed "simulated" wrestling activities such as scramble drills, position drills and situation drills for use during the early weeks of the season. I rarely allowed live action to extend beyond half a minute and commonly limited it to ten or fifteen seconds.

By the time we entered our mid-season practice mode (Appendix 3) our live wrestling periods had a duration of two minutes or longer and single periods of ten minutes or more were not unusual. Our situation wrestling periods were also extended and when we wrestled full matches they included three periods of two minutes each plus a full overtime.

As we transitioned from mid-season to late-season mode I routinely scheduled two or three practices where our wrestlers warmed up, selected a reasonably competitive partner and then wrestled live for an hour or longer without a break. Wrestling steadily for an entire practice taught our kids to pace themselves and to vary the intensity of their effort as they wrestled. It was a particularly convincing way to teach the effectiveness of following intervals of controlled action with explosive scoring maneuvers. The matches also toughened our wrestlers physically and mentally and we discovered that their pride in accomplishing such a formidable task dramatically boosted their self-esteem and confidence. During these extended matches, with the exception of bleeding, non-stop action was required and the practice room walls were considered "in bounds".

Situational wrestling

I am a great believer in situational wrestling. Placing wrestlers in a particular position and wrestling a fifteen second to one minute period provides the opportunity for them to develop proficiency at recognizing and executing the offensive and defensive techniques that the position affords. In our program we discovered that situational wrestling was a particularly effective means of elevating our wrestler's overall effectiveness with certain techniques. If we felt that we had been ineffectively using our far-side cradles, then we had one wrestler lock his partner into a cradle and we started live action from that position. Similarly, if we were having difficulty countering a single with efficiency, we placed one man in a single-leg, instructed his partner to apply a whizzer and wrist counter and wrestled from that position. Requiring our wrestlers to wrestle from a particular position (i.e. a bar arm, a half nelson, a sit back position, a fireman's carry, etc) always produced dramatic improvement in their effective use of those techniques in competition.

The various circumstances that can be practiced by designing situational wrestling drills are limited only by the creativity of the coach. In our program I utilized situational wrestling for many purposes but I found that it was particularly helpful in teaching our wrestlers the techniques and strategies that were most effective when they found themselves in positions or circumstances that demanded quick thinking and confident action.

Explosion Drills

The short, timed bursts that I referred to as explosion drills were among the most effective means of improving our wrestler's technique and efficiency from the bottom position. After signaling the technique that I wished the defensive man to execute, action was initiated on the whistle and a live period of from five to fifteen seconds ensued. At times, the offensive wrestler was allowed to wrestle freely and, in other instances, he was told to simply hang on and "ride". An escape or a reversal ended the period and the partners quickly switched positions and the drill was repeated. This procedure provided many full speed repetitions in a very short span of time and greatly improved our explosiveness and efficiency in coming off the bottom. It also helped our wrestlers to develop techniques for maintaining control of a desperate and explosive opponent.

My team particularly enjoyed explosion drills when the loser was required to do push-ups. When the wrestling period ended the losing wrestler was required to do ten push-ups, lowering his chest to touch his partner's fist. The defensive wrestler earned push ups if he failed to score from the bottom and the offensive wrestler earned them when the defensive man was successful in scoring an escape or reversal. If there was disagreement about who won, both men had to do push ups. Using push-ups as an incentive always led to spirited competition and ensured maximum effort.

Over-working

It is common for coaches, in their zeal to prepare and toughen their wrestlers, to push them to exhaustion at the beginning of the season. Following the example of my high school coach I initially made the same mistake but a few seasons of experience illustrated that fatigue was hindering rather than accelerating my wrestlers' progress. There are important reasons for coaches to thoughtfully plan their conditioning program, particularly as it relates to the early season. First, as a result of being pushed too hard too soon, many inexperienced recruits will quit before they attain a level of fitness that allows them to cope effectively with the rigors of practice. Second, the focus in early season practices must necessarily be upon technique instruction and fatigued wrestlers are poor learners.

An additional conditioning error relates to the tendency of coaches to push too hard for too long. This approach can be particularly destructive

115

because when the physical rigor of each day's practice is unrelenting, many athletes will burn-out both physically and mentally. In actuality, physical conditioning is similar to putting salt on your food. The right amount can make a dish taste better but too much salt ruins it.

While I was coaching at Alaska's Chugiak High School in the 1970's my teams were large and included many mature and gifted athletes. One of those teams was particularly remarkable. They had been rated highly in a national pre-season poll and we were in our third year of an unbeaten streak that eventually stretched to sixty four dual meets. As I approached what was certain to be a brilliant season, I reasoned that if one practice a day was good then two would be better. Further, I decided that we could also gain an additional edge by working our hardest from the first day of the season to the last. I even scheduled demanding drill sessions in the hours before our meets. The results were predictable; my highly motivated athletes, rated at the very top of the state wrestling polls for the entire season, ended up physically and emotionally drained and we took a disappointing second in the state tournament.

After that season ended the monumental proportions of the coaching blunder that I had committed finally dawned on me. The lesson

116

learned, although harsh, was effective and, from that point forward, I attempted to pace my teams' development. I had learned to place restraint upon my desire for immediate success and to focus, instead, upon steady improvement.

Specifically, in my post-Chugiak season plan, the development of my wrestlers' technical abilities, and in later years their positioning skills, became the emphasis in early season practices. I had learned that steadily developing a solid base of fitness through a system of progressive conditioning and drilling was far superior to "putting the pedal to the metal" for the entire season. Predictably, this shift in approach was accompanied by a higher rate of retention and more rapid learning but there was also a negative associated with it. Because it took us longer to achieve a fitness level appropriate for competition we often suffered a slight decline in our level of success during early matches. For me the trade-off was well worth the price. Early season disappointments were seldom remembered when measured against our post-season accomplishments.

My Chugiak experience had also taught me the value of including an adequate amount of "rest" and "fun" in my practices. Those adjustments proved to be crucial in promoting the development of the highly desirable attitudes and level of effort that I sought to cultivate in my wrestlers.

118

CH 10
Peaking

During the first fifteen years of my coaching career, other than working my wrestlers as hard as possible and arranging for a tough competitive schedule, I gave little thought as to how I might help them achieve a late-season performance peak. I simply knew that peaking at state would be the best of all possible accomplishments. Simplistically, I assumed that "peaking" would be the natural result of a season of sustained effort. That approach proved frustrating, however, because during those early years my teams and wrestlers often peaked prematurely. Eventually, however, trial and error and observation of some truly outstanding programs and coaches revealed that with forethought and planning I could increase the probability that my team would peak appropriately in the post-season.

Peaking Physically

A few years ago, at a clinic in California, I listened to Lehigh University Coach Greg Strobel (6) speak convincingly about the importance of planning practices with an appropriate balance between "volume" and "intensity". Coach Strobel shared his conviction that an artful balance between the two was required when a coach desired to successfully peak his team. As he spoke I realized that my own experiences had led me to very similar conclusions. My only regret was that I had not heard him years earlier.

In planning a season schedule that will produce a late-season peak the most essential task is to design a practice schedule that reflects an evolving and artful balance between practice volume (length) and intensity (physical effort). I found it most effective, in terms of achieving a late-season peak, to emphasize instruction and de-emphasize physical conditioning during early season practices. As a result my early practices were high in volume and low in intensity. As the season progressed, however, I gradually shifted to progressively higher levels of intensity as I reduced practice volume. Those adjustments culminated with post-season practices that were only sixty to ninety minutes in length.

Because that approach forced my team to begin competition before they had developed a desirable level of physical fitness it became important to communicate to our wrestlers and to their parents that our early season focus was on effort and improvement rather than winning. I found it helpful to describe my approach as analogous to ascending a very long and steep staircase by taking a single step at a time. Explaining that we viewed each successive competitive event as an opportunity to make progress toward the goal of being at our very best at the end of the season, I was usually able to placate all but the most demanding of fans.

As a result of placing primary emphasis upon progress and improvement, when early season disappointments did occur, this explanation helped to minimize their negative impact. Our wrestlers knew that we wanted them to give one hundred percent effort in each and every match but they were also aware that we did not expect them to be in post-season form until they reached the post-season.

To reinforce this approach, I often made a large line graph displaying my evaluation of each of our performances and posted it in the wrestling room. This proved to be a particularly effective way to visually illustrate team progress and to reinforce the assertion that although occasional dips in performance would invariably occur that our plan would, over time, produce consistent, steady progress. The display of improvement illustrated by the graph always seemed to help us to build to a peak and to affirm our wrestlers' expectation that they would be at their very best at state.

In addition to adjusting volume and intensity, providing an adequate amount of rest during the course of a season is also essential to the attainment of a post-season peak. Wrestling is incredibly demanding, both emotionally and physically, and wrestlers will progress more rapidly, maintain higher levels of enthusiasm, avoid burnout and ultimately achieve more success if they are given an occasional day off.

As a young coach I was slow to recognize the value that a day of rest could have in accelerating my team's progress. Finally, however, I realized that pushing too hard, too soon and for too long had been preventing the achievement of the very goals that my practice schedule had been designed to accomplish. After a few years I began to build planned rest days into our season schedule and I found that Thanksgiving and Christmas holidays were, in particular, important times for our wrestlers to enjoy their families, travel or just kick back. Rather than detracting from our peaking effort these short breaks were consistently successful in renewing my wrestler's enthusiasm and in sharpening their focus on the post- season.

As an unexpected dividend of giving my wrestlers time off for the holidays parents became more supportive of our program and often expressed appreciation for my willingness to allow their family to have a break from the rigors of the season.

I also used our twice weekly, fifty minute study table to reduce the volume of practice during the first two-thirds of the wrestling season. The practices that followed study table were shorter, but they were intentionally designed to be more intense. Following a Study Table practice it was not unusual for wrestlers to approach me with comments like; "That was such a great practice coach, the time just flew by! Or "Geez Coach, I can't believe it but I lost eight pounds in an hour and a half!"

In general, coaches should always be on the look out for signs of "burn out" or indications that their team is getting "stale" as the season progresses. When such signs are noted it is time to make an adjustment. As Coach Strobel stated in his California presentation; "We have to learn to read our guys!"(6) It can be difficult to respond appropriately to a team's need for a break but I can assure you that when it is necessary it well worth doing.

The "more is always better" philosophy is deeply ingrained in most of us, but I have found that over-training is a sure way to peak too soon and that appropriately decreasing practice volume and providing opportunities for needed rest and recovery is absolutely essential to achieving a timed peak.

Peaking Psychology

If, as coaches, we fail to motivate our wrestlers, prepare them for the adversity that they will all experience and teach them the techniques that will help them to win in the battle of wills with their opponents, then our neglect will limit their potential for success. If we are to successfully guide them to a timed peak then we must focus on mental and emotional preparation as well as on the development of their technical skills and stamina.

When a coach explains his vision and shares his goals for the season with his team it is the perfect opportunity to begin preparing them to peak at state. Goals can be immensely powerful in guiding and shaping behavior and coaches are well advised to select those that they embrace with care.

If, for example, a goal is established that places undue emphasis on achieving some lesser accomplishment, then that goal can actually diminish the probability that a wrestler or team will peak at state. Admittedly, my observations regarding the relationship between peaking and goal setting are at best subjective. However, nearly forty years of coaching experience has served to convince me that the unintended consequence of establishing an achievement other than peaking at state as a primary goal is all too often an early peak and post season disappointment.

I once worked alongside a dedicated and capable basketball coach who almost exclusively focused his team, season after season, upon winning

124

the league championship. In fairness, his teams had compiled an impressive string of league titles but they were consistently frustrated by, and criticized for, a seemingly inexplicable string of post-season collapses.

Similarly, for close to a decade, my team faced a rival with an unprecedented string of regional championships. Each year the back of their team t-shirt touted their ever-expanding chronology of regional titles and affirmed their focus on adding another to their inventory. I can recall my frustration at never being able to wrest a regional title from their grasp but those memories are considerably diminished because of the frequency with which my team finished ahead of them in the state tournament.

Each of these programs was phenomenally successful in achieving their primary goal but they often ended their season in frustration. Had either coach established a post-season peak as the ultimate goal in his program, I have little doubt that it would have been achieved.

Creating focus is also critical in the effort to direct a team toward achievement. The motto of the wrestling team at tiny Warden High School in Washington's Columbia Basin is "Place at State". (1) Under the tutelage of long time coach Rick Bowers, Warden has strung together an amazing record of post season achievement for more than a decade. Many factors including good coaching, a tradition of excellence and community support have contributed to Warden's success. It is their team motto, however, that has served to focus those elements, leading them with amazing consistency to what is for Bower's wrestlers, the ultimate goal.

Two of the surest ways for a coach to focus his wrestlers on doing their best at state include sharing inspirational stories about former wrestler's successes and directing his team's attention to the examples of public recognition found in their school and community.

After the subjects of my stories had graduated, I am certain that every wrestler on every team that I ever coached heard about my first state champion Don Barnum, about Pete Imhoff shifting from 185 to heavy for the post season and winning an improbable state championship against a three hundred and twenty pound opponent, about Terry Simpson capturing third at state and boosting his team to a state title after he cracked several ribs in the regional tournament, about Ed Peppers coming from twelve points behind in less than two minutes to win a one point decision and a state medal, about Ray Rodriquez entering the state tournament as our JV entrant and winning a state title, about Terry Zapien winning four consecutive matches at state with pins in a total of less than six minutes and many, many others.

At Chugiak High School every wrestler on my team began his freshman year dreaming that he would, through his wrestling exploits, one day be able to add his name to the Wall of Fame in our wrestling room.

In Zillah, at both the east and west entrances to the community, large, wooden signs immortalized each of the State Championship teams the community had fostered. For years prior to winning our first state title, my assistants and I felt driven to ensure that one day wrestling would be added to the list of venerated teams emblazoned upon that sign and we made sure that our wrestlers felt the very same way. We also paraded our entire team into the gymnasium to contemplate the banners hanging high on its walls. It was almost a spiritual experience for our kid's as we reviewed the name of every wrestler who had ever placed at state for Zillah. I have absolutely no doubt that many dreams of glory solidified into resolve during those powerful moments.

Most wrestling coaches recognize the critical role that physical conditioning plays in their wrestlers' success but, all too often, mental preparation is ignored or left to chance. This seems an unlikely paradox because wrestling coaches

127

almost universally will acknowledge that mental preparation and toughness are needed for success in their sport. My conclusion is that many either fail to recognize the importance of mental preparation or that they feel unsure about how to approach designing a truly effective program for its development.

It had always seemed logical to me, given its potential value, that I should strive to identify or develop techniques to train my athletes' minds as well as their bodies. In particular, I determined that strategies that could instill confidence in my wrestlers, strengthen their will to persevere in the face of adversity and create focus in pursuit of their goals would be particularly desirable.

In the effort to create a program for improving our wrestlers' "mental toughness" I identified five traits or skills that I felt were closely associated with acquiring and demonstrating that quality;

➤ An ability to establish reasonable long and short term goals, design strategies for their attainment and effectively evaluate personal progress.

➤ A willingness to prepare, to physically extend themselves on a daily basis and to take pride in the effort to outwork their opponents.

➢ Extraordinary self-discipline that allows them to extend their personal quitting point beyond normal limits and to persevere in the face of personal setbacks.

➢ The willingness to embrace and utilize, in practice and in competition, techniques designed for gaining a mental edge, including; an attack mentality, a stubborn refusal to relinquish points and a commitment to displaying an extraordinary level of fitness

➢ The disposition to have confidence in their coaches and in their own resolve and the ability to successfully establish, pursue and achieve their goals.

With these abilities in mind, I designed strategies, selected techniques and formulated instructional drills that would provide opportunities for repetitive practice in each area. We also developed, posted and frequently referred to a number of team "slogans" that served to reinforce the traits and attitudes that we desired our wrestlers to reflect in their psychological preparation, including:

➢ You deserve to win. You have worked harder, longer and smarter than your opponents!

➢ Never give up! Make your opponent quit first!

➢ Refuse to give points!

- Don't just prepare. Prepare to beat the best!
- A loss always will hurt, but it is a great opportunity to identify and eliminate your weaknesses.
- Beat your opponent mentally and you will beat him on the scoreboard!
- We love overtimes!

One of the most successful aspects of our effort to ensure that our wrestlers were emotionally prepared for the stresses and unpredictability of competition was that we consistently took the time to discuss the various opportunities and pitfalls that could be encountered in a match and to practice techniques and strategies for dealing with them.

By designing activities and drills in which our wrestlers could practice reacting appropriately to those situations they often gained a decided advantage over their opponents. It was a strategy that proved its worth on many occasions. Some of the drills we developed emphasized the following situations;

- following every takedown with an immediate pinning combination
- fighting off scoring attempts and creating stalemates rather than allowing points to be earned

- reacting to being taken down by exploding into an immediate bottom series
- exploding on the edge of the mat in anticipation of an opponent's relaxation
- sprinting back to the middle of the mat from out of bounds in an effort to project energy, intimidate an opponent and influence the official
- strategies specifically designed to allow a come from behind victory in every possible situation
- maintaining control of an opponent while avoiding stalling penalties
- maintaining a positive focus despite a questionable call by an official or negative behavior by an opponent
- developing the toughness and discipline necessary to bounce back from an emotional loss when minimal recovery time is available

Using these drills and many others we discovered that we could effectively teach our wrestlers to meet potentially unexpected or negative situations with greater confidence. Each also proved to be valuable in our yearly push toward a post-season peak.

Cutting Weight

It also seems appropriate, when discussing attitude and mental preparation, to comment on the impact that cutting weight can have on the peaking process. Some of the most difficult decisions of my coaching career were associated with wrestlers who were cutting too much weight or doing it improperly.

In most situations providing a wrestler with assistance regarding nutrition and counseling him and his family about the dangers of excessive weight loss helped to resolve the problem. In a few cases, however, more drastic action was necessary.

Linda and I frequently had kids to our home for dinner on the night before a match. We made sure that they ate a healthy meal and they often slept over because it reduced the temptation to eat or drink during the night. On a number of occasions, when all other approaches had failed, I forced a wrestler to move up a weight. In almost every instance I encountered significant resistance from the wrestler and his parents but, eventually, they came to the realization that it had been in his best interests.

When wrestlers compete at or very near their natural, conditioned body weight they learn more rapidly, remain more positive, are less likely to suffer injury or burn-out and their ability to achieve a post season peak is enhanced.

Peaking Frequency and Duration

Years of experience led me to conclude that, as a general rule of thumb, a team can peak at its maximal potential just once during a wrestling season and that a peak can be maintained for no more than three consecutive weekends.

Embracing that premise does not preclude the possibility of a team or individual achieving other notable successes on the road to a post-season peak but it does provide a caution against pushing too hard, too soon and for too long. Before adopting this philosophy I had coached several teams and a number of individuals who had suffered disappointing, late season performances after having reached exhilarating heights during the regular season. Once I embraced the concept of striving for a single, late-season peak, however, we were consistently at our best at state.

Building Confidence

Athletes and teams gain confidence when they experience success in competition but when confidence develops as a result of extraordinary dedication and effort, particularly when it has been voluntary, it is especially powerful.

For many years I used a "Two Hundred Miles to State" program to encourage my wrestlers to show a level of dedication above and beyond the norm. In doing so, those who chose to participate

133

set themselves apart and, by season's end, had gained the confidence and determination that only extraordinary effort can produce.

We charted each participant's progress and displaying it prominently in our practice room. Wrestlers were required to accumulate at least twenty-five miles of extra running before their name was added to the chart and then they were allowed to record their own progress in five mile increments. At least once each week we reviewed the chart in practice, praising the participants and encouraging others to join them. In addition to the obvious physical benefit gained as a result of their involvement, those who participated also came to feel that they had "paid the price" and deserved to make it to state. It was unusual for a wrestler who completed the two hundred mile challenge to fail in their effort to qualify.

CH 11
Dual Meet Strategies

From the perspective of many fans a dual meet is wrestling at its most exciting. Even those who have little understanding of technique and scoring are easily caught up in the ebb and flow of the action, the swings in momentum and the suspense provided by a closely contested dual.

Besides the action on the mat, a dual meet can quickly develop into a sort of "human chess" as coaches shuffle their line-ups and use various other strategic ploys in an attempt to out-maneuver each other. When effective, such tactics can produce improbable victories and leave hapless opponents stunned.

My initial exposure to the use of strategy in dual meets proved to be both frustrating and humbling. As a rookie I often found myself pitted against and outwitted by much more experienced coaches who were brutally effective in their use of strategy to expose my inexperience and neutralize my team's strengths. By making ample use of the element of surprise and various nuances in the rules they moved their men around like chessmen and, all too frequently, they were successful in the effort to keep us off balance. Unsettling and upsetting my team and I with their maneuvers, they routinely weighed-in multiple competitors at a single weight and made my wrestlers feel like it impossible to prepare themselves for competition. They made liberal use of their prerogative to shift their men to higher weights at the last moment, leaving us befuddled and vulnerable. When match procedures required their wrestler to report to the mat first, they simply waited for my over eager wrestlers to rush to the mat ahead of them and then they calmly inserted a different wrestler or chose to forfeit. Feinting when they wished to avoid a particular match-up, they sometimes sent a wrestler toward the mat and when we responded by sending our man out, they simply withdrew their wrestler before he had fully committed and sent out a replacement.

On more than one occasion my wrestlers and I were left feeling like the proverbial "rug" had been pulled out from under us!

In my youthful naiveté, I recall being excited about spotting one of our league's most experienced coaches in the bleachers at a home dual. A week later I learned that his presence had a "dark side" because his scouting prowess allowed him to identify and take advantage of my team's weaknesses and devise effective strategies to counter our strengths.

All the early experiences I have described were harsh and they were often infuriating but I soon came to admire and emulate the men who had administered those painful lessons. As the years passed I also came to realize how very fortunate I was to have been exposed to and allowed to rub shoulders with no fewer than five men who have since been inducted into Washington's Wrestling Coaches' Hall of Fame. Each became a legend in his own community, contributed to my education as a coach and padded his win loss record at my expense.

The coach of a team that is clearly superior has little need to strategize. In the event that a team is closely matched or an underdog, however, a coach using strategy can significantly improve his team's potential for an upset.

When a coach intends to employ strategy in a match it is best to be judicious in sharing his plan with his team. The old adage that "loose lips sink ships" is particularly applicable to the use of strategy. I will never forget the wrestler who loudly asked me, while standing in a weigh-in line prior to an important dual, whether he was supposed to be weighing in at 152 or 160. A day earlier I had explained to him that I planned to weigh him at 152 and shift him to 160 in an effort to freeze our opponent's tough 152 pounder and take advantage of a weak freshman at 160. Because my regular at 160 was even weaker than our opponent's freshman, and because their 152 pounder could easily dispatch ours, I figured that we could escape with a split if I shifted him up and forfeited at 152. Needless to say, my wrestler's poor memory and ill-advised inquiry foiled my intentions. Providing too many specifics can easily thwart the planned use of strategy, particularly when an excited wrestler forgets his role or fails to keep what he knows to himself.

For the most part, when I planned to employ strategy in a match I spoke in generalities to my team providing little information that could tip my hand to our opponent. When I planned a shift I simply indicated that we might be bumping up and left it at that. In some cases more information was necessary. When I wanted to create a specific match-up, for example, I made certain that my wrestler knew exactly why I wanted to pit him against the opponent and what I expected him to do.

When it seemed likely that an opponent would use strategy against us or could effectively gain advantage by doing so, I routinely cautioned our wrestlers about that possibility. Discussing the potential for its use eliminated the element of surprise and served to minimize the impact of strategy when it was employed against us.

Training our wrestlers to get themselves ready to wrestle rather than to gear up for a specific opponent was also an essential part of our preparation for a dual meet. Focusing on an specific opponent can be valuable but when the potential exists for a last second change in a match up it makes little sense and can even work to a wrestler's disadvantage. Because it was a standard procedure on our team to weigh-in all of our available wrestlers at every weight prior to a dual, preparing to wrestle rather than to face a specific opponent was a strategy that served us well. It allowed me to move my wrestlers in and out of the line-up at will and gave us a degree of flexibility that was unavailable to many of our opponents. I also recognized that weighing everybody in made it more difficult for opposing coaches to predict our intent and, best of all, it gave them one more thing to worry about. It was a useful ploy.

In an additional effort to disguise my intent when I planned to employ strategy in a match, I required every wrestler who weighed in at a specific weight to begin a simultaneous warm-up at least two matches prior to competition at their weight. A lone wrestler warming up behind the bench can be a dead giveaway when opposing coaches are attempting to anticipate a line-up shift. Of course, the potential also exists to mislead the opposing coach by warming up the "wrong" wrestler.

Because a strategic move is often countered with a corresponding adjustment by the opposing coach, I also required all of our wrestlers to remain behind our team bench until I personally instructed them to report to the table for their match. To ensure that they followed this directive, and to guarantee that all of our wrestlers began their warm-up at the appropriate time, I made it a practice to assign an assistant coach to monitor the warm-up area.

Over the years using of strategy produced some exciting and unexpected victories for my teams. As a case in point, at Clover Park we employed various strategies to defeat the same league opponent for three consecutive seasons. In each meeting we had been a decided underdog but by shifting our line-up and creating unexpected match-ups we were able to keep our opponent off balance. We also forfeited to their most outstanding wrestler each season so that we could prevent him from supplying his teammates with the momentum that his dominating performance was certain to have provided.

One of the most memorable dual meet victories of my entire career also came about because I employed strategy in an unexpected way in a high profile match. I was coaching at Chugiak High in Alaska and I had gone to considerable trouble to scout our undefeated opponent during the weeks preceding our match. Kenai had an outstanding team that season and it was obvious to me that our chances of beating them were pretty slim, particularly if we went straight at them with our regular line-up. No matter how I shuffled things, it still came out in Kenai's favor and so I decided that our best chance for a victory might be to create an unexpected match-up.

As I reviewed their team, weight class by weight class, it occurred to me that we might possibly gain some advantage if I moved our 132 pounder away from Kenai's returning state champion. Bumping him up looked like it would produce a sure win for us at 140 and help us escape with a split at those two weights. Faced with a decision to forfeit or send out a "sacrificial lamb" against their champ, I decided that I would move a tough, unorthodox and virtually unknown sophomore into our varsity line-up at 132 to face him. I hoped that our kid's unusual style might prove frustrating to his opponent and that, with his innate toughness, he might be able to survive the match without being pinned.

The day of the match we had to travel several hours by bus to reach Kenai and when we departed Chugiak I informed the two wrestlers who were to be involved in the shift of my plan. I cautioned them about discussing our strategy with their teammates and told them to begin preparing themselves mentally for their matches. Arriving at Kenai I weighed both of them in at 132 and at 140 I weighed-in our regular. Duals always began at 98 pounds in those days and by the time we reached 132 we were still holding our own in the hotly contested match. As Kenai's state champion took the mat at 132 to the approving roar of their very partisan crowd I remember sheepishly shoving our sophomore out to face him, just hoping that he could hold out for six minutes. When the match ended the only noise in the gymnasium came from our team bench as the stunned Kenai team and crowd watched the referee elevate our sophomore's arm in victory! Our regular at 132 quickly dispatched their 140 pounder in the next match and with the impetus provided by those two wins we rolled on to most unexpected victory. Our win later proved to be the only blemish in Kenai's state championship season.

I have encountered a few coaches who genuinely resent the "gamesmanship" involved in using strategy. Although I respect the right of each man to his own opinion regarding its use, and have understood their chagrin when their team has suffered an unexpected loss because of it, I strongly disagree with those who decry the tactical use of strategy as unethical. Employing strategies that are permitted by the rules is an element of virtually every competitive sport known to man and I have never understood why some feel that wrestling should be an exception. Having been on both the receiving and dispensing ends of the effective use of strategy, I have always considered it to be a "part of the game". Coaches who choose to use it, however, should be aware that they risk incurring the animosity of the opposing coach when their strategy works effectively.

144

CH 12

Developing Team Leaders

Once a coach recognizes the benefit that can be derived by providing leadership training to his wrestlers and by empowering them with real responsibility, he will waste little time in implementing a leadership development program.

It doesn't take many years of coaching experience to discern that each team has its own personality, that some squads are blessed with outstanding natural leadership and that others suffer from its lack. Neither does it take many seasons to recognize the powerful correlation that exists between effective leadership and success. Less obvious, however, are the steps that can be taken to ensure that the leadership potential possessed by each new season's team is fully developed.

Team Captains

The most obvious student leaders on any wrestling team are its captains. Captaincy is often bestowed upon the most successful or most dedicated of a team's seniors and, when they happen to be effective leaders, their positive impact can be substantial.

Just prior to and following my retirement, I volunteered as a part-time and then fulltime assistant in my oldest son Glen's wrestling program

145

in Ripon, California. During each of those seasons Glen's squad included a typical mix of seasoned veterans, mid-level wrestlers and raw beginners but the work ethic, attitude, team spirit, rate of progression and success achieved by one of the teams easily outstripped that achieved by the others. Revealingly, the leadership on the most highly achieving team had been exemplary and had been provided by a group of highly motivated seniors. Leading by both word and example, their support for the values and work ethic that they had been taught by their coach produced a season of accomplishment for the entire team.

Because of the nature of their role, captains can have a particularly powerful influence upon their team's success. Selecting them then becomes a vitally important process. My staff and I initiated our selection each year by preparing a list of worthy nominees. Those we nominated were usually seniors and most were exceptional wrestlers. More importantly, however, those we nominated had demonstrated their leadership potential by displaying maturity, an exemplary work ethic, a positive attitude and a concern for the welfare of their teammates. Self-absorbed or selfish wrestlers are never great captains. After we had pared our list of nominees to a reasonable number, usually four to six, our team selected the two or three that they

146

favored by secret ballot. We announced the results at our end of season award banquet and our captains served for an entire year. Our system of selecting captains had three distinct advantages:

- ➤ First, graduating seniors were able to vote thus reinforcing our emphasis upon senior leadership and ensuring that their maturity would be reflected in the outcome.
- ➤ Second, because they had been selected from among the list of nominees by democratic vote they always seemed to enjoy the support of their teammates.
- ➤ Third, our procedure allowed ample time for us to provide leadership experiences and training so that our captains could grow into their roles.

Once our new captains had been selected, I immediately involved them in the process of establishing team goals, developing our tournament schedule and selecting new uniforms and a summer camp. I also made sure that they understood that they would be expected to be the hardest workers in our practice room, show total commitment and dedication in their pursuit of excellence and fully embrace and reinforce our coaching philosophy.

During the season they were assigned to direct the daily preparation of our mats, plan and lead warm-ups, supervise pre-practice shower and skin inspections, direct post-practice locker room clean-up and provide leadership in preparing and cleaning the gymnasium before and after our matches. I also asked them to monitor compliance with the school's athletic code and do their best to keep their teammates out of trouble. I consistently sought their input in matters of individual and team discipline and they were encouraged to rove the space behind the team bench during dual meets; monitoring sportsmanship, exhorting their teammates and assisting in their pre-match preparations. During tournaments our captains organized team support whenever we had a wrestler on the mat and assisted us in the corner when we were short-handed.

Empowering young men with real responsibility always encourages them to develop into effective leaders.

Senior Leaders

It was one of my assistants at Zillah that first opened my eyes to the power of senior leadership. Coach Daniel Robillard's description of his own high school experience and the empowerment of seniors leaders by his coach was vivid and convincing.

Responding to his suggestion I assigned a couple of seniors to act as advocates for the freshmen and sophomores on our team and another to monitor team sportsmanship. Another was asked to compile a selection of appropriate music that we could use in our practices during grass-drills and live wrestling and still others accepted assignments to assist in the preparation of our team highlight video. After creating as many roles as were needed to empower each senior it soon became apparent that placing them in positions of leadership had been a stellar move. Led by our seniors our team's spirit and attitude was better than it had ever been. As a result, I continued to utilize seniors as team leaders throughout the remainder of my career.

Challenging Athletes

Despite working to create a family atmosphere and to value the contribution of each member of our team, I usually found that there were a few wrestlers who resisted our effort to guide them in a positive direction. Tellingly, most of the problems we encountered with attitude, attendance or training during the season also originated them.

Suspending a problem athlete from your team is never easy but the consequence of failing to consistently enforce team rules regarding the possession or use of illegal substances, theft, poor sportsmanship, irregular attendance or other significant infractions is always destructive to a program.

A problem athlete's reluctance to "buy in" is seldom resolved without a significant expenditure of time and energy. It can be tempting to cut your losses and to give up on such individuals, particularly when they have reached the point where their presence on the team has become a significant liability. Wrestling can, however, by its very nature be a particularly powerful change agent and molder of character.

In light its power to modify behavior I often chose to work, for a time at least, with those wrestlers who had poor attitudes or were guilty of lesser indiscretions. The awareness that dedicated coaches had, in the past, guided countless wrestlers into productive paths and lives as responsible adults influenced my decision to continue to work with such individuals. I would like to be able to say that, in the majority of such cases, I was ultimately successful in helping them make the adjustments that allowed them to become productive members of the team but, in actuality, I experienced many more failures than successes and most problem athletes eventually quit or were removed.

There were, however, some notable exceptions and, like so many other coaches, it is those successes that motivated me to continue the effort. The story of Jose is unique but it illustrates, perhaps more effectively than any other that I could share, the value of empowerment and the role that leadership responsibility can have in effecting change in a dysfunctional wrestler's life.

Jose

Jose seemed to be a hopeless case. He was a tough kid from a single parent family and, with his mom working long hours, he had few restrictions or controls on his behavior or activities. He had been a poor student in junior high and he frequently seemed to be involved in, or on the fringe of, the negative events that occurred in our school. His belligerence and poor attitude had earned him a reputation as a trouble-maker and so I was surprised to see him show up for wrestling during his ninth grade year.

During that first season I eventually removed Jose from the team because of his repeatedly erratic attendance. However, as a sophomore he once again expressed interest in wrestling and came out for the team. Despite his professed desire he was, without any doubt, one of the laziest and least coachable kids on our squad. Predictably, although Jose attended most practices, he made very little progress during his second season.

He showed up again during his junior year and demonstrated a greater willingness to work hard and, as a result, he began to make progress in attitude and ability. As a result, Jose began to

151

experience success but his performances were at best spotty and each of his losses was characterized by a display of poor sportsmanship. I consistently disciplined him for his negative outbursts but, although he always completed the penalties I assigned for his infractions, he showed little willingness or ability to restrain his unacceptable behavior.

As a senior Jose seemed to be a different kid. He showed an improved attitude, a terrific work ethic and he was incredibly motivated. Despite the evidence that he was now one of the hardest workers on our team, his past behavior had blinded his teammates to his leadership potential and he had been bypassed in our selection of captains.

As we helped each wrestler to establish his season goals that season I recall being dubious about Jose's written assertion that he would work hard enough and long enough to win a medal in the state tournament. He had little post-season experience and, in his only previous opportunity to wrestle beyond the district level, he had failed to make weight on the first day of the regional tournament.

As our season progressed, however, Jose put together an impressive string of victories. I was ecstatic, both with his successes and with the changes that he seemed to have made in his life. It

152

was at that point that he lost his first match and his temper!

The official was barely able to get Jose to comply with end of match procedures and, as he returned to our side of the mat, he slammed his headgear to the floor. Immediately approaching him I made it clear that his behavior was unacceptable and that in our next practice he would pay dearly for his display of poor sportsmanship.

Jose did the extra work I assigned him without complaint but a few matches later, in another losing effort, he again lost his temper. Once again, I pulled him aside but this time I told him that I wanted to see him after the match when the team had finished cleaning-up the gymnasium and locker rooms.

Jose was sitting at the base of the bleachers, by himself, when I finally came out of my office that night. Everyone else had gone home for the night and as I sat down beside him I asked him if he understood how bad he had made himself and his team look? He seemed to understand but he expressed the conviction that the anger that he felt following a loss was uncontrollable.

As I explained that he had run out of chances and that the next time he lost his temper I would have no other option but to kick him off the team, an incredible idea simply popped into my head. I said; "Jose, I could, just like last time, give you half an hour of extra grass-drills as a punishment for your poor sportsmanship but I don't think that it will do any good. What do you think I should do?" Jose's response was to simply shrug his shoulders and so, I said; "I am not going to give you the extra work, instead, I am going to require you to sit and watch as I make the team do the grass-drills that you earned with your poor sportsmanship!"

The impact of my statement on Jose was not what I had anticipated. Immediately, tears began to stream from his eyes and he jumped up and shouted, "You can't do that!" My response was immediate. I told him that I not only could do it but that I was going to. His outrage apparent and his face and eyes reddened with emotion, Jose looked as if he was about to explode and he screamed; "then I quit!" My response; "Go ahead, they're going to do your grass-drills anyway!" was delivered as he stormed out of the gymnasium and ended our exchange.

I didn't expect Jose to show up on Monday, but he did. He sat, listening and watching, as I explained what was going to happen and why to his teammates. As the entire team struggled through the next thirty minutes of pain, the anguish on Jose's face was indescribable. By the time they had finished and I had dismissed them to the locker room, humility had replaced the belligerence of the previous evening and it was then that I implemented the second phase of Jose's "punishment". I told him that I was putting him in charge of team sportsmanship and, as awareness of what I was suggesting dawned upon him, Jose looked as if the weight of the world had been dropped upon his shoulders.

I explained that giving him the responsibility for sportsmanship would require him to be an example and to hold himself to the highest standard of acceptable behavior. Then I assured him that I was confident in his ability to do the job. I also told him that if it became necessary for him to personally address a display of inappropriate behavior or poor sportsmanship on the part of a teammate that I would support him, just as long as the punishment was appropriate and administered fairly.

During the next few weeks Jose's reaction to his new assignment was amazing. He became a leader, not only in fulfilling his responsibility for team sportsmanship but in all other ways as well. Never again did I have to speak to him about losing his temper and, as the season progressed, I often observed him counseling various members of the team concerning their conduct.

At the end of that senior season Jose qualified for the state tournament and, in a string of amazing upset victories, he captured fifth place and the state medal that he had coveted.

Jose's accomplishments and growth that season convinced me of the amazing power that bestowing leadership responsibility can have in turning a man's weaknesses into strengths. It was a lesson that I never forgot.

CH 13

Assistant Coaches

The familiar old saying that "folks tend to support that which they help to create" is an essential element in developing a successful working relationship with your assistant coaches. Assistants deserve to be assigned duties that reflect their interests and abilities and, if they perceive those assignments to be meaningful, they will give the best that they are capable of giving.

Empowerment fosters initiative, it generates respect and appreciation and it ensures effort but, as a head coach, you must always be willing to shoulder the responsibility for providing the instruction and guidance that is necessary for your assistants to perform optimally.

During my years as a head coach I worked with at least sixteen different paid assistants and dozens of volunteers. The vast majority had a love for wrestling and a passion for coaching. Unfortunately, until I had experienced both the frustration of working for a coach who lacked an understanding of empowerment and the satisfaction of serving with another who made ample and effective use of it to motivate, energize and strengthen his assistants, I failed to understand its

157

power. As a result, I am certain that most of my assistants spent their years in quiet frustration.

It was not until I became an assistant for my friend Steve Wolfe in Homer, Alaska that I discovered that empowerment was one of the secrets to effectively utilizing assistant coaches. As Steve's assistant I was given real responsibility and provided with the assistance, training and support that I needed and then, most importantly, he stepped back and allowed me to do my job. Steve was equally quick to share the accolades that accompanied his team's successes, making each of us feel that our contributions had been acknowledged and appreciated.

Juxtaposed with my experience serving as an assistant for Steve, during one of my stints as an assistant football coach, I learned first hand what an assistant feels like when he has been disenfranchised. During the early weeks of that football season, despite my assertion that I lacked adequate knowledge and experience to work effectively with our team's defensive ends, our new head coach gave me that assignment and expressed confidence that I would be able to perform it effectively.

Starting with a knowledge base somewhere near zero, I invested a great deal of time and effort in preparing myself. I read everything I could find about playing and coaching the position of defensive end and asked questions of the other coaches. Our head coach was so busy with his other duties that he was usually preoccupied or unavailable when I sought his input and so I was forced to implement the things I had had learned in the absence of his advice or counsel.

During our first game it was apparent that our defensive ends were performing miserably. Frustrated by their poor showing I had anticipated that the head coach would provide me with the advice and instruction I needed to coach them more effectively. Instead, without explanation, he simply reassigned the responsibility to another staff member. I was devastated and remember that I left the coaches' meeting feeling as though I had been grounded for a month by my father. The remainder of the football season was marred by staff unrest and chaos both on and off the field and our frustrated team lost every game. My decision to decline the offered assistant's position for the following year was an easy one.

My experiences, both good and bad, eventually taught me to empower my assistants and from that point forward I attempted to give them real responsibility. I also did my best to create a supportive, non-threatening atmosphere in which they could work and flourish. By making meaningful

159

assignments, offering a listening ear, providing instruction and assistance, expressing appreciation for effort and sharing the credit for successes my staff and my team prospered.

There were a few instances over the years when I felt compelled to release an assistant prior to the end of the season. In each case I sought their discharge because I believed that their inappropriate conduct presented a clear danger to our athletes. In situations where their deficiencies were less threatening, I attempted to provide them with the counsel and training that they needed. Only rarely, when a substantial commitment of time and effort had failed to produce the necessary improvements, did I recommend non-retention of such individuals.

CH 14

Boosters

Boosters groups can be valuable allies in a coach's effort to build a quality wrestling program but they can also become his greatest nightmare. Despite having experienced both ends of the spectrum I have found the benefits of working alongside supportive parents and community members to be worth both the effort and the risks.

A well organized, helpful and hardworking Boosters Group can relieve a coach of the burden for fund-raising and can provide a level of support that far exceeds that provided by most high school athletic budgets. In an effort to minimize the potential negatives of working with Boosters, however, the following suggestions are offered:

- ➢ Be selective in seeking and cautious in accepting funds from Boosters. There are usually strings attached.
- ➢ Avoid involvement with "blanket" Booster groups. Such groups are well intended but they are often less than even handed in their support for the various activities that they purport to represent.
- ➢ Consistently avoid discussing coaching strategies, personnel decisions or staffing issues with or in the presence of Boosters.

Failure to follow this admonition always creates dissention and jeopardizes the health of your program.

One of the best ways to ensure that a Boosters' Club functions in an appropriate manner is to personally lay the ground work for it by organizing it yourself. By beginning the effort with a suggested constitution and bylaws the entire process can be accelerated and many pitfalls can be avoided. It is essential when writing bylaws that they specifically state that the coach's role in the organization will be advisory in nature. Listing a coach as an officer or member of the organization is fraught with danger because it can expose him to accusations of impropriety. By designating the coach as an advisor, he is relieved of the responsibility for handling club monies and precluded from authorizing club expenditures. Both features protect his reputation.

I have seen a number of careers end tragically because coaches failed to appreciate the dangers associated with handling and spending Boosters' funds. It is a near certainty that those who ignore the potential risks associated with such activities will continue to suffer similar consequences.

Starting a New Booster Group:

For those who wish to start a Boosters' Club, following these steps and giving consideration to the suggestions included with them may prove to be helpful:

- Meet with parents at an announced organizational meeting or at your pre-season banquet. Make a short presentation on the formation and the purpose for the organization and assess the level of interest. Identify a committee of five or six parents who are willing to work with you to develop an organizational plan. (Caution: Starting with a group that is too large can make this step difficult.)
- Schedule a committee meeting for the immediate future.
- Prior to the committee meeting prepare a rough draft for a suggested constitution and by-laws. The proposed document should include the name and purpose of the organization, a listing of officers and their duties and a provision regarding meeting frequency. (Appendix 5)
- The draft constitution should contain provisions for the election of officers and for making amendments to the constitution and it should clearly state the number of members

that must be present to constitute a quorum. These are all areas that will eventually create problems if they are not included.

➢ The by-laws should identify the coach as an advisor and specifically prohibit him from voting or accessing the organization's funds without authorization. (Appendix 5)

➢ The committee should review and modify the proposed constitution as deemed desirable and present it for group consideration.

➢ Following adoption of the constitution and bylaws the Athletic Director should be provided with a copy and informed of the purpose and structure of the organization.

➢ Ask your A.D. for advice and guidance and certify that you will not be serving as an officer or voting member in the organization. That will allow support to be more freely given to your effort.

➢ Provide your A.D. with the assurance that you have clearly communicated the necessity of School Board approval to the Boosters and that they fully understand the necessity of securing approval prior to conducting fund-raising activities or representing themselves as a school-affiliated organization.

➤ Inform the School Board of the Boosters intent to apply for non-profit status and seek their approval of the organization's charter. Once board approval has been granted and officers have been elected, submit the completed application for non-profit status to the State.

166

CH 15

Working with Athletic Administrators

The simplest approach to establishing a solid, working relationship with an athletic administrator or principal is to communicate frequently and effectively and to comply with all requests for input and paperwork in a timely manner. By working hard to ensure that your wrestling program is highly organized and that your requests for resources and time are well-justified and reasonable, you are likely to develop a mutually beneficial relationship with your athletic administrator. On the other hand, coaches who behave as if their program is at the center of the universe and who make demands rather than requests soon find that their relationship with their administrator has become strained.

Managing a school's activities can be a complex and daunting task and coaches who do their jobs quietly and efficiently, with sensitivity to the demands of the A.D.'s position and a willingness to see the big picture, will find that they become valued employees. I have known a few coaches who have viewed such professionalism as somehow subservient or "brown nosing" in nature but my view is that it is not only the right thing but the smart thing to do.

Because of my willingness to work cooperatively with my athletic administrators I was, with a single exception, consistently successful in developing a mutually beneficial relationship. My effort to responsibly comply with proscribed guidelines and regulations was also recognized and appreciated and, as a result, I enjoyed a high level of trust and was given a great deal of freedom as I worked to develop my wrestling program. It was equally gratifying to discover that when I erred in judgment or inadvertently failed to follow proscribed procedures that my miscues were met with understanding and a willingness to view them as the honest mistakes that they truly were.

The best advice I can give to coaches who wish to establish rapport with their athletic administrator is as old as the Golden Rule. Treat your boss the way you would like to be treated and courtesy, communication and cooperation will make a good working relationship possible.

Ch 16

A Final Reflection

After more than forty years I can still scarcely believe the good fortune that led to me to become a high school wrestling coach.

Although I had always enjoyed participating in sports, I had never seriously considered becoming a coach until I was interviewed and hired as a science teacher and wrestling coach at Warden High School. It was a miracle of sorts and one for which I will always be grateful.

My father's dream was that I would become a dentist one day but, instead, I chose to follow my heart into education. I am grateful that dad chose to support me in that decision but I'm not sure that he ever really understood the amazing blessings that would be associated with life as a high school teacher and coach.

Each time a former wrestler contacts my wife Linda and I to thank us for the difference that they feel wrestling, and our association with them, has made in their lives, I think of dad's dream and I try to imagine how often a dentist hears the words; "Remember when you filled that molar? It changed my entire life!"

Appendix 1
Coaching Philosophy

As coaches:

- ➤ We will demonstrate in everything that we do that the focus in our wrestling program will be on the development of an exemplary work ethic, responsible behavior and leadership. We will use the unique power of wrestling to turn boys into good men and responsible citizens.

- ➤ We will strive to be consistently positive and healthy role models for our athletes. Our actions will reflect integrity, self control, responsibility, personal accountability and an exemplary work ethic.

- ➤ We will appropriately empower those we work with; our fellow coaches, team leaders, responsible parents and fans to contribute in meaningful ways to the wrestling program.

- ➤ We will consistently demonstrate that we value each individual who displays the courage and willingness to commit to the sustained effort that is necessary to become a wrestler.

- ➤ We will consistently communicate and demonstrate that family needs trump the demands of the wrestling program in the lives of our wrestlers and coaches.

➢ We will respect and show support for all school activities and we will teach our wrestlers to do the same. We will demonstrate flexibility in honoring our wrestlers' commitments to other programs.

➢ We will promote wrestling in every possible way and be willing to expend our personal time, energy and resources in the promotion and development of our program and the sport of wrestling.

As a team:

➢ We will place heavy emphasis upon the mastery of basic techniques, learning all moves in series when possible. It will be our intent to achieve a level of technical proficiency that will enable us to score effectively from all positions against all opponents.

➢ We will drill at least thirty minutes per day in an effort to develop muscle pathways that will allow us to react automatically to the various positions and situations that we may encounter in competition. We will work to develop the ability to "chain" wrestle.

- We will work hard enough so that we can be confident that we are out-working our opponents but we will exercise patience as we progressively build our physical fitness to ensure a late season "peak" in our performance.
- We will embrace the concept of "blue collar" values and work to earn everything that we receive. We will clean up after ourselves, show appreciation and lend support to those who need it. We will be humble in victory and graceful in defeat. We will neither display nor tolerate poor sportsmanship.
- We will maintain good body position during competition, eliminating error and making it difficult for our opponents to score. In addition, we will develop techniques that force our opponents out of position and make them vulnerable to attack.
- We will be aggressive initiators in all positions, placing a particularly heavy emphasis upon offense, attacking and pinning. We will strive to be an exciting team for spectators to watch.
- We will work to develop and display a mental toughness that is characterized by our refusal to quit or give up. We will fight every effort our opponent makes to score. We will hustle

and develop an "in your face" attitude when on the mat. We will work to extend our quitting point and never concede victory until a match has ended.

- ➤ We will seek out the toughest possible opponents possible, placing heavy emphasis upon tournament competition, as we prepare for the post-season. The achievement of post-season excellence, including placing at state as individuals and as a team, will become our hallmark and tradition.

Appendix 2
Season Plan

CP Wrestling
2003-2004 season

Saturday Nov 1ˢᵗ Coaches work out 8am, Coaching Families BBQ at noon
*Monday Nov 3ᵗʰ- Rules Clinic 6:30 pm
*Tues Nov 4ᵗʰ- Pre-season meeting for wrestlers
Fri/Sat Nov 7ᵗʰ & 8ᵗʰ Staff at State Coaches Clinic
*Mon Nov 10ᵗʰ Staff attends pre-season League Meeting
*Sat Nov 15ᵗʰ- Coaches Meeting 8am-noon topic: preseason preparation: warm-up, gear, weigh-ins, cleaning, score-keeping, skin inspection, split practice format, assignments 8am-2pm
(note: 12 separate days of practice are required before wrestling in a dual, 10 days for a Jamboree)
Mon Nov 17ᵗʰ – Season begins (mat cleaning, skin inspection, locker room clean-up, showering, practice schedule, lockers, washing gear, head gear, skin inspection, weigh-ins, security for valuables, chiropractic permission and wt certifications, spirit packs, study table) (scrubbing walls and mats) 3-5:30 pm
Tues Nov 18 practice IA JV 2:45-5:15 & V 5:00-7:30pm
Wed Nov 19 ½ day Practice IA   4-6:30pm (everyone together)
Thu Nov 20 practice IA JV 2:45-5:15 & V 5:00-7:30
Fri Nov 21 practice IA   "
Sat Nov 22 practice 8am-11am (everyone together)
Mon Nov 24 practice IA 2:45-5:15 & 5:00-7:30pm
Tues Nov 25 practice IA "
Wed Nov 26 no practice
Thu Nov 27 no practice
Fri Nov 28 practice IA 1:00-3:30 pm "Challenges"
Sat Nov 29 (TD Jamboree 10 am) & Banquet 4 pm
Mon Dec 1 practice IA   2:45-5:15
Tues Dec 2 study table practice IB   "
Wed Dec 3 practice IA   "
Thu Dec 4 study table   CP @ Washington 5:15 & 7pm
Fri Dec 5 Varsity travels to Bellingham   JV Practice IA 3-5pm
Sat Dec 6 @ Bellingham Duals, JV Tourney @ Auburn
Mon Dec 8 practice 2A 2:45-5:15
Tues Dec 9 practice 2B 2:45-5:15
Wed Dec 10 CP @ Lindberg 5:15 & 7pm

Thu Dec 11 study table *Fife @ CP* 5:15 & 7pm Favorite Staff Member Night

Fri Dec 12 practice 2A (Varsity travels to RA Long for practice) JV Practice 3-5pm

Sat Dec 13 V @ R.A. Long Inv   .JV Tourney @ Franklin Pierce

Mon Dec 15 practice 2A 2:45-5:15

Tues Dec 16 study table   practice 2B   "

Wed Dec 17 practice 2A   "

Thu Dec 18 study table CP @ White River 5:15 & 7pm

Fri Dec 19 practice 2A 2:45-5:15 and set up mats

Sat Dec 20 Hall of Fame Duals at CPHS 9am

Mon Dec 22 practice 2A 8am-10:30 am

Tues Dec 23 practice   (60 minute match)

Wed Dec 24 no practice

Thu Dec 25 no practice

Fri Dec 26 no practice for varsity   C Tourney at North Mason

Sat Dec 27 Varsity practice 2A 10am   JV Tourney @ North Mason

Mon Dec 29 CP @ Pacific Coast Inv in Vancouver
JV practice 2A 9am-11am

Tue Dec 30 CP @ Pacific Coast Inv in Vancouver JV practice 2A 9am

Wed Dec 31 V Practice 2A 9am...no JV practice

Thur Jan 1 V practice 2A 9am...no JV practice

Fri Jan 2 V @ Sequim Inv *JV practice 2A 9-11 am*

Sat Jan 3 @ Sequim Inv *JV practice 2A 9-11am*

Mon Jan 5 practice 2A 2:45-5:00

Tue Jan 6 practice 2B   "

Wed Jan 7 practice 2A   "

Thu Jan 8 study table   Peninsula@ CP 5:15 & 7pm (Alumni Nite)

Fri Jan 9 practice 2A 2:45-5pm & set up mats for JV tourney

Sat Jan 10   JV Tourney @ CP 9am

Mon Jan 12 practice 3A 2:45-5:00

Tue Jan 13 sprints 6:30 am   practice 3B 2:45-4:45pm

Wed Jan 14 practice 3A "   "

Thu Jan 15 study table   CP @ Lakes 5:15 & 7:00 pm

Fri Jan 16 Sprints 6:30 am practice 3A 2:45-4:45 pm (JVs travel to Concrete)

Sat Jan 17 V practice 3A 8:00am (90 minute match) JV Tourney @ Concrete   *C Tourney @ Olympia*

Mon Jan 19 practice 3A 2:45-4:15 pm

Tue Jan 20 sprints 6:30 am study table practice 3B 2:45-4:30 pm

Wed Jan 21 sprints 6:30 am   practice 3A   "
Thu Jan 22 study table Franklin Pierce @ CP 5:15 & 7pm (Parents Night)
Fri Jan 23 V Travel to Spokane   JV practice 3A 2:45-4:30 pm
Sat Jan 24 @ Dream Duals in Spokane JV Tourney @ Timberline 9:30
Mon Jan 26 practice 3A 2:45-4:15 pm
Tue Jan 27 sprints 6:30 am practice 3A 2:45-4:15 Varsity only   (JVs & C at Rainier 7pm)
Wed Jan 28 study table Seamount League Championships 7pm
Thu Jan 29 Sprints 6:30 am,   practice 2:45-4:00 pm (60 minute match)
Fri Jan 30 practice 3A 2:45-4:00 pm & set up mats for Tourney
Sat Jan 31 JV "All Comer's Tourney 10am-3pm" (practice 8am-9:30 am)
Mon Feb 2 Sprints 6:30 am   practice 3A 2:45-4:00 pm
Tue Feb 3 Sprints 6:30 am study table practice   3A   "
Wed Feb 4 Sprints 6:30 am   practice   3A   "
Thu Feb 5 study table   practice   3A   "
Fri Feb 6 District Tourney @ CPHS
Sat Feb 7 District Tourney @ CPHS
Mon Feb 9 **no practice**
Tue Feb 10 sprints 6:30 am practice 3A 2:45-4:00 pm
Wed Feb 11 sprints 6:30 am practice 3A   "
Thu Feb 12 sprints 6:30 am practice   3A   "
Fri Feb 13   practice   3A   "
Sat Feb 14 Regional Tourney @ White River vs. Metro
Mon Feb 16 sprints 8am practice 8-9:30 am 3A (no school this wk)
Tue Feb 17 sprints & practice 3A   "
Wed Feb 18 sprints & practice 3A   "
Thu Feb 19 practice @ Tacoma Dome
Fri Feb 20 State Tourney @ Tacoma Dome
Sat Feb 21 State Tourney @ Tacoma Dome
Banquet- Sat March 14th 3pm-7pm (CPHS)

Appendix 3
Practice Plan Modalities

Early Season Mode (prior to the 1st tournament)
IA: Full Practice Days (2 ½ hours)

Warm up & stretching: 20 min
Position Drills: 5 min
Ropes/chin ups/push ups: 5 min
Review/ Drill: 10 min
Instruction: 20 min *
Review/ Drill: 10 min
Instruction: 20 min
Break-2 min
Review/Drill: 10 min
Instruction: 20 min**
Simulated Wrestling Activities: 10 min
Drill/Condition: 20 min
*A portion of this segment can be used for warm-up, or drill early in the season. **This instructional period can be deleted and replaced with live wrestling once all technique has been taught.

IB: Study Table Days (2 ½ hours)

On study table days we deleted the ten minute position drill, up to ten minutes of conditioning and thirty minutes of instruction or drill in order to accommodate the forty-five minute study table and five minute passing time.
WU & stretching- 20 min
Position Drill: 10 min
Drill/Review: 10 min
Instruction: 20 min
Wrestle: 20 min
Break-2 min
Condition: up to 20 min

Mid-Season Mode (first Tournament to mid January)
2A: Full Practice Days (2 hours)

WU & stretching: 15 min

177

Ropes/chin-ups/pushups: 10 min
Slow Roll: 10 min
Drill: 30 min
Break- 5 min
Wrestle/condition: 50 minutes

2B: Study Table Days (2 hours)
Study Table and passing time: 50 minutes
WU & stretch- 15 min
Drill: 20 min
Slow roll/wrestle: 15 min
Condition: 20 min

Late Season Mode (mid-January through the State Tournament)
Sprints 6:30-6:50 am in morning

3A: Full Practice Day 1 ½- 1 ¾ hours or less

WU & stretch- 15 min
Instruct/Talk/Review/Slow roll-5 min
Drill- 30 min
Break- 5 min
Wrestle- 30 min
Conditioning- 0-20 minutes on non-sprint days
On sprint days this period was eliminated, however, those who missed morning sprints were required to do 20 minutes of 3 second drops after practice.

3B: Study Table Days 2 hours or less
Study Table and passing time- 50 minutes
WU & stretch-15 min
Drill- 20 min
Slow Roll- 5 min
Wrestle- 30 min

Appendix 4
Strict Drill Sequence

<u>On the Feet:</u>
Firemans Carry from inside tie and push
Knee tap
Wheel
Syracuse
Crusher
Barrel Roll (outside drop)
counter by controlling wrist
block crotch
Double (face drag)
Submarine
Crack Down
Front Headlock
Butt Drag
Ankle and Cradle
Spin and Shuck
Cross-face near ankle lift and spin
Single- he ties to head (change off to double)
Single-fake—turn corner to finish
Spin single
High Single to Spladle
Whizzer & Wrist vs Single Leg
Whizzer & Alvarez
Whizzer and Quarter Nelson
Quarter Nelson and Long Arm push thru

Whizzer..side by side...man steps over

He hits whizzer and you come up to both feet and double trouble
Roll thru whizzer
Limp arm whizzer
High Crotch from head snap
High Crotch from elbow trap
Howdy duck & hazard
Drag to go behind
Snap and Spin
Under-hook to Throw-by
Under-hook to Throw-by and Pick (ankle or knee)
Under-hook and Sit
Hook-up & Lateral (dump)

Snap to knees and Head and Arm
Head and Arm counter from standing- Lock and Drop back
Head and Arm counter on mat (chase the leg, lock & roll)

On the Top:
TWAC (Tight waist arm chop) to Head Lever
Near TWAC (near and far) to Two on One and drive
Far TWAC

Far TWAC to Two on One and drive
QP (Quick Ankle Pick)
QP to Far Knee Far Ankle and Half Nelson
QP to TWAC to Near Cradle & drive
QP to TWAC to Two on One and drive
Two on One to Cheap Tilt (Kip)
To Navy and drive

Navy..he hand fights..hook and suck-back
Hook and Cheap Tilt

To Near Cradle and drive
To Cheap Tilt
To Far Side Half Nelson
Opposite side Two on One to Half Nelson
Spiral
Bar drive
Bar bone
Bar stack
Half Nelson
Half Nelson Stack
Near Cradle and drive
Bridge-back Cradle
Far cradle and Rip
Rip and Roll
Counter with arm through and post
Crossbody and Roll when head is grabbed
Force-half
Counter: Tripod and Roll
Knee to Chest & Arm Thru

Rear Standing:
Lift and Dump and cover opponent's legs
SPS (Step, Pull, Sweep)
Kip

180

On the Bottom:
Stand-up and Heist
Stand and Switch (fake and go)
Stand Sweep-Roll
Sit Back and Stand
Sit and Head-pull
Sit, Heist and Peterson
Sit-, turn in and Crayfish
Sit, turn in to Peterson Roll
Switch
Switch, Sit and Roll
Back-hook (or post to mat) and step over counter to Switch

Other Takedown Set-ups:
Inside tie to chop double
Face in or spin down
Shoulder pop to double
Head Snap to double
Slip Squat and knee bounce
Inside tie to wax off and High Crotch
Shoulder pop to High Crotch

Defense:
Down-block, snap & spin
Down-block to Front Head Lock
To Butt Drag
To Cradle
To Jitney
Cross-face, near ankle & spin

Appendix 5
Boosters Constitution and Bylaws

I.   <u>Name</u>: The name of the organization shall be the _____Wrestling Boosters

II.   <u>Membership</u>: Membership is available to all interested individuals age 18 and older who are interested in the promotion of wrestling at _____High School and its feeder schools.

III.   <u>Purpose</u>: The promotion of excellence in the wrestling program through fundraising, advertising, sponsorship of camps, trips and other promotional activities shall be the prime mission of the organization. The organization will play no role in program, coaching or administrative decision making, nor will they have input in selecting personnel.

IV.   <u>Meetings</u>: General Meetings will be held on the first Tuesday of each Month at 7 pm. Additional meetings can be convened by approval of the Executive Chair and any two Executive Board members, based upon need or in response to a request by a member.

    Executive Board Meetings may be called by the Executive Chair at the request of any Executive Board Member or the Advisory Coach. They may be attended only members of the Executive Board and the head coach.

V.   <u>Executive Board Officers</u>: The organization's officers shall be:

    1) <u>Executive Chair</u>- conducts the monthly meetings, coordinates the organizations efforts and organizes the agenda.

    2) <u>Financial Chair</u>- coordinates the fundraising efforts of the organization and keeps the financial records.

    3) <u>Executive Secretary</u>- keeps accurate minutes of all meetings, and distributes them to all Executive Board members.

    4) <u>Promotions Chair</u>- coordinates the effort to assist and promote success in the high school wrestling program and in its feeder programs. This is includes coordination of the effort to provide workers for wrestling events.

    5) <u>Communications Chair</u>- in the effort to ensure the organizations success develops a communication system which will inform, invite and promote participation by all

community members. (A newsletter is recommended for this purpose.)

VI.   Advisory Coach:
The Head Wrestling Coach will serve in a non-voting advisory position and will be responsible to plan and implement, with the assistance of the Boosters, an improvement plan to promote excellence in the wrestling program.

VII.   Changes in the Bylaws: Proposed changes to the by-laws must be presented at a regularly scheduled monthly meeting and must be approved by more than fifty percent of the members present to qualify for consideration at the next regularly scheduled meeting of the organization.
When the vote is conducted, a simple majority will be required for proposed changes to be adopted.

VII: Voting: Only members in good standing may vote during the organization's meetings.
Good standing is achieved as the result of having attended at least one of the previous two general meetings. The Executive Secretary will distribute a list of those entitled to vote at the start of each meeting.

VIII: Approval of Financial Expenditures: The Executive Board may approve expenditures of five hundred dollars with the approval of three Executive Board members.
With the above exception, all financial expenditures must be approved by a simple majority of those in good standing at a regularly scheduled meeting of the organization.

IX: Yearly Updates: After consultation with the Board, the Executive Director will propose house-keeping and other changes in the Bylaws at the September meeting each year.

X.   Yearly Plan: After consultation with the Board, the Financial Chair and the Advisory Coach will present a one year plan for consideration and approval each September. The plan should include all long range goals or projects and should outline the fundraising needs of the organization. The membership will vote to accept, reject or modify this plan.

XI.   Checking Account: All Executive Board Members will be included on the signature card and will be authorized to sign checks; however, two signatures will be required. The Financial Chair will be in possession of the check book and the Advisory Coach may not be a signatory.

Citations and Credits

1. Bowers, Rick. Place At State. Warden High School.

2. Mikovich, Mike. 1977. The Mike Milkovich Practice schedule For High School Wrestling Coaches. Mike Milkovich Enterprises, Inc. 53 p

3. Owens, Marge. 1970. "They Work For What They Want". Warden Register.

4. Seibel, Ron. 1996. Unpublished Notes. Washington State Wrestling Coaches Association Fall Clinic.

5. Spies, Connie. 1969. Its Takes A Sport Like Wrestling. Unpublished Poem.

6. Strobel, Greg. 2003. Unpublished Notes. Monterey Clinic of Champions. Monterey, California.

7. Wolfe, Steve. 2002. The Five Point Philosophy. Wrestlingconsultants.com. 104p.

8. National Federation of State High School Associations. 2008. www.nfhs.org/

About the Author

Darrel White was born in Tacoma in 1946 and grew up in the small, western Washington town of Montesano. In high school White and many of his schoolmates were first introduced to wrestling by football coach Dick Watson. Watson lacked knowledge of the sport but he knew how to get a team in shape and, as a result, Montesano experienced a modest level of success during his tenure. Interestingly, both of the co-captains in 1964, White and his best friend Mike Turner became wrestling coaches.

Coach White attended Grays Harbor Community College in Aberdeen, Washington where he received an A.S. in Biology in 1966 before transferring to Western Washington and then to Central Washington University where he earned his B.A. in 1968 and M.Ed. in Biology in 1973.

As newly-weds, White and his wife Linda relocated to Warden in 1968 where, at the age of 21, he was hired as a high school science instructor. White was also convinced by the Superintendent of Schools to restart the wrestling program. Wrestling was considered a "major sport" in Washington's Columbia Basin but Warden had, much to the chagrin of the community, been without a wrestling program for several years. While at Warden Coach

White established a youth program and led the high school team to a 7th place finish at state.

After three years at Warden, White was hired as a biology instructor and wrestling coach at Mt Edgecumbe High School, a Bureau of Indian Affairs boarding school for native students. in Sitka, Alaska. While at Mt Edgecumbe, White and several other Southeast Alaska wrestling coaches established the Alaska Wrestling Coaches Association. Following his two year stint at Mt. Edgecumbe White accepted a position as biology instructor and head wrestling coach at Chugiak High School in the Anchorage School District.

While teaching and coaching at Chugiak the Whites became the parents of three children Glen, Chance and Glee. In each of the nine years that he was at the helm of the Chugiak program White's teams finished in the top eight in the state tournament, winning one state championship and claiming three second place finishes. Coach White also served as president of the Alaska Wrestling Coaches Association while at Chugiak and was named Alaska's first Coach of the Year in 1978.

Accepting a position as Assistant Principal and Athletic Director at Homer in 1982 White coached Junior High wrestling for one season and assisted Steve Wolfe, first as a volunteer and later as an assistant, during a span in which Homer won a state title and became the dominant small school wrestling program in Alaska.

Prior to leaving Alaska, White joined his life-long friend and fellow coach, Mike Turner, as an elected member of the Alaska Wrestling Hall of Fame.

Returning to Washington in 1989, White was hired as a biology instructor and head wrestling coach at Zillah High School. In eleven years at Zillah, White and long time assistants Daniel Robillard and Manuel Torrez, with the support of Junior High Coaches John Mitchell, Andy Kelly and Hal Phillips, built Zillah from a virtual unknown into a Washington Class A wrestling powerhouse. In six of his nine final seasons at Zillah, White's team placed eighth or higher in the state tournament, finishing as runners-up in 1995 and capturing back to back state titles in 1999 and 2000.

Coach White was selected as Washington State A/B Wrestling Coach of the Year in 1983 and as overall Washington State Wrestling Coach of the Year in 1998. He also served as team leader for Washington's 1998 cultural exchange tour to Japan and as Director of the Washington State Wrestling Coaches Hall of Fame for five years. Elected President of the Washington State Wrestling Coaches Association in 1998 White served for two years in that capacity, later serving as past-president and for two years as a member of the WIAA Coaches Advisory Board.

In 1999 Coach White accepted a position at Clover Park High School in Lakewood, Washington. In 2000 he was named National Federation of High Schools Wrestling Coach of the Year for Section 8 (Northwestern United States).

White's final four seasons as a head coach were spent at Clover Park where his tenure was highlighted by the revitalization of the wrestling program and by his 2003 squad's fifth place finish in Washington's AAA State Tournament.

During his career White coached 28 state champions and a total of 122 state place winners. In 2006 he was inducted into the Washington State Wrestling Coaches Hall of Fame.

Coach White retired as a teacher and coach in Washington in 2004 and volunteered for two seasons as an assistant coach in his son Glen's wrestling program in Ripon, California. White and his wife Linda are the proud grandparents of four grandchildren; Brent, Victoria, Ryker and Rylee and they now reside in the small town of Brownsville, Oregon.

LaVergne, TN USA
30 August 2009
156431LV00004B/144/P